"The child is father of the man."

— WORDSWORTH

"In the children lies the seed corn of the future."

— FROEBEL

"Who touches the child touches the most sensitive point of a whole which has roots in the most distant past and climbs toward the infinite future.

"Who touches the child touches the delicate and vital point where all can yet be decided, where all can be renewed, where all is pulsating with life, where the secrets of the soul lie hid.

"To work consciously for the child and to go deep down, with the tremendous intention of understanding him, would be to conquer the secret of mankind, just as so many secrets of Nature have been conquered in the world about us.

"The activity of the child has always been looked upon as an expression of his vitality. But his activity is really the work he performs in building up the man, it is the incarnating of the spirit."

— MONTESSORI

"But Jesus said to them, 'Let the little children be, and do not hinder them from coming to Me, for of such is the kingdom of heaven.'"

— MATT. xix, 14.

THE MONTESSORI REVOLUTION IN EDUCATION

THE MONTESSORI
REVOLUTION
IN EDUCATION

E. M. STANDING

SCHOCKEN BOOKS · NEW YORK

First SCHOCKEN *edition 1966*

Copyright © 1962 by E. M. Standing

Published by arrangement with The Academy Guild Press, Fresno, California.

Library of Congress Catalog Card No. 66-14877

Manufactured in the United States of America

INTRODUCTION

A REVOLUTION IN EDUCATION

Every great revolution, every great movement which stirs the minds and souls of men, has its focus, its representative, its interpreter. Thus Aristotle summed up the knowledge of the ancient world as St. Thomas Aquinas did that of the Middle Ages. Similarly Francis Bacon, with emphasis on inductive logic, came to be regarded as the founder of modern science, while the name of Charles Darwin has become synonymous in many minds with the idea of evolution. In the same way, the historian of the future will look upon Maria Montessori as the representative and interpreter of a great social movement which centered, and still centers, around the child.

For, in spite of the fact that two world wars have taken place in it, the century in which we live has often been called the Century of the Child. This is not without justification, for in no previous epoch of history have so many organizations for child welfare come into existence. In Montessori, more than in any other single individual, this movement so characteristic of the *Zeitgeist* of our time has become luminously self-conscious. What others felt vaguely or in disconnected fragments she was able to see as a whole, discerning the movement in its general outline and direction. In her, aspirations which were stirring in the hearts of millions the world over found articulate expression.

Montessori's appeal was essentially to the spirit; and in this she was in contrast to many of the psychologists and pedagogues of her day. "A teacher," she always maintained, "must not imagine that he can prepare himself for his vocation simply by acquiring knowledge and culture. Above all else he must cultivate within himself a proper attitude to the moral order. Especially must he purge his soul of those two mortal sins to which teachers are particularly prone—pride and anger." This appeal to the spirit explains the extent of her influence over such a variety of persons of differing age, religion, color and civilization. There was something in the depth, sincerity and certitude of her vision, and the authority which came with it—in her noble conception of humanity with its cosmic mission—and most of all in her own personality which seemed to cast a spell on those who came in contact with her.

Many of those did come, literally, from the ends of the earth to attend her famous international training courses, and were surprised at the effect this experience had upon them. They came simply expecting to hear lectures on child psychology, the training of children, the teaching of various subjects, the management of children, and so forth. All these things they *did* receive in ample measure. But, as the months passed by, they began to be aware that something else was happening too, something they had not expected; something different and more valuable, which they would have found difficult to put into words. They came with the intention of learning to help the child in his development and, to their surprise, they found that they were being unexpectedly helped in their *own* development. Subjects which they had disliked at school suddenly acquired a new and absorbing interest. New horizons were opening up before their minds, not only in the realm of the intellect but in the very meaning and scope of education. They experienced a genuine enlargement of mind and soul, and knew themselves, at the end of the course, to be different and greater than they were at the beginning. They realized that they had made a spiritual investment which would yield them interest as long as they lived—because life had taken on a new meaning and a richer promise.

E. Mortimer Standing

CONTENTS

LIST OF ILLUSTRATIONS

PART ONE
MONTESSORI PRINCIPLES

Without any doubt we have in the past been the unconscious oppressors of this new human seed which bursts forth pure and charged with energy. And we have superimposed ourselves upon it without admitting the needs of its spiritual expansion. So the child has remained almost completely hidden — or very much overshadowed — by this unconscious egotism of the adult. It would be an affirmation not too well received, I imagine, were I to say that very often the adult becomes an obstacle, rather than a help to the development of the child. It is a most difficult thing for us to accept the statement that, very often, it is our excessive care for the child which prevents the exercise of his own activities, and therefore the expansion of his own personality . . .

Thus it comes to pass that when we, with the very best intentions and with the most sincere wish to help, do everything for the child — when we wash him, lift him up and plunk him down on his chair, feed him, and put him into that species of cage we call his crib — in giving him all these unnecessary aids we do not really help but hinder him.

And later on, towards the boy or girl, we repeat the same error, when — still holding to the belief that he cannot learn anything without our help — we stuff him with intellectual nourishment, we nail him to the benches of the school so that he cannot move, we make every effort to uproot his moral defects, we crush or break his will, secure in our belief that in this way we are are acting for his highest good.

And so we proceed in this manner indefinitely all along the line; and we call this education.

MARIA MONTESSORI

CHAPTER ONE

THE FUNDAMENTAL PRINCIPLES OF THE MONTESSORI METHOD

NO ONE CAN FULLY APPRECIATE THE MONTESSORI METHOD by simply studying its principles in the abstract. That is why Montessori would never grant even a preliminary diploma in her method to any student, however brilliant, unless, in addition to the theoretical work, that student had also spent many days observing the principles in action in a recognized Montessori school. And then, only after two years spent successfully in practicing the method, could the full diploma be obtained. It is the lack of any such firsthand acquaintance with Montessori principles *in action* which explains why learned persons, including certain professors of education (who had never been inside a Montessori school), so completely misunderstood it.

Speaking of learned professors reminds the writer that, many years ago when he was giving a series of lectures in Germany, he was informed that "the prospects of the extension of the Montessori method in Germany were very slight because a recent conclave of German psychologists had decided against it." This gloomy prophecy did not, however, impress him in the least; because, in the long run, it will not be German or any other professors who will decide the question. It will be the children themselves.

3

This brings us to the first point we wish to emphasize with regard to the principles of the Montessori method, viz., that they are founded directly on the laws of life itself. It is no exaggeration to say that this method has the vitality of a living thing; for it is based, directly, on the observed manifestations of a living thing — the human child.

It can be safely asserted that Dr. Montessori has already taken an assured place, with Froebel, Pestalozzi, Comenius, etc., among the great educators of history. But, from another point of view, we might as justly claim that Montessori has also made a name for herself among the great biologists of all time — with Darwin, Mendel, Fabre, de Vries, and so on. Her method of research was substantially the same as that of the biologists. Very similar, too, was its aim because, like theirs, her study was concerned with the spontaneous manifestations of organisms. She clearly realized that her success was due to this biological method; and compares it in particular to that of the great French naturalist, Fabre, "the Homer of the insects."

"Fabre," she said, "did not take his insects into his study and experiment with them there. Rather he left them free in the environment most suited to them; and — without letting his presence in any way interfere with their natural functions and mode of living—patiently observed them until they revealed to him their marvelous secrets."

Thus it was with Dr. Montessori. She realized that neither the ordinary nursery school, nor yet the environment of the home, had been made to suit the needs of the child. And so, if one may use the paradox, she *created* a *natural* environment for the child (that is, one suited to his nature). Then, while other people talked about the necessity of giving children freedom in education, she actually provided them with it.

At the same time, with an unrivaled power of observation, she studied their free behavior in this new environment and discerned its significance. Indeed, one could sum up the Montessori method by saying that it is a *method based on the principle of freedom in a prepared environment.*

It is this intimate connection between the principles of the Montessori method and the laws of biology which led Professor Godefroy, professor of psychology in the University of Amsterdam, to express himself as follows:

> "Those who are not favorable to the Montessori method ask, skeptically, what will become of it after a number of years, implying that before long a new system will have taken its place.
>
> "It is not difficult to explain to such that the Montessori method is founded on the general characteristics of life, proper to all organisms, and that it will last as long as life itself lasts. It is not possible to imagine that such a principle, having once been introduced into pedagogy, could ever be abandoned."

This also explains why the Montessori method has had such instant success wherever it has been properly applied, irrespective of climate, race, religion or social distinctions; and why it still continues to make fresh conquests, often in spite of determined opposition.

THE MONTESSORI METHOD NOT A CLOSED SYSTEM

The Montessori method is not a closed system, discovered once and for all, henceforth to be applied unchangingly. It is continually growing like a living thing, growing in depth, richness and variety. Those who studied it forty, twenty or even ten years ago would be surprised to find how much more there is in it now than there was then. This applies not only with respect to the wider application of its principles, but also with regard to the depth of those principles themselves. The more one studies them, the more one finds in them to study.

The reason for this is twofold. In the first place, these principles, based on the profound and secret forces of life, are as limitless as life itself; and secondly, on account of the extraordinary genius of the founder of the system.

It was the writer's privilege to have worked for more than a quarter of a century in personal contact with the *Dottoressa*. As the years passed, the conviction steadily deepened that she possessed an intuitive insight into the soul of the child so clear, so immediate, so simple, that she could never hope fully to explain it, or pass it on to others. There is, in fact, something about the nature of all genius, in whatever sphere it operates, which suggests the power to move in a fourth dimension, something at once simple and unconstrained, yet incomprehensible and incommunicable.

Although Dr. Montessori gave more than thirty international training courses to teachers, she never gave the same course twice. She was always breaking new ground. In every fresh course she approached her subject from a new angle and developed her lectures around a new *leitmotif*. One year it would be the idea of freedom; another, the spiritual training of the teacher; or, again, it might revolve around the difference between work and play; or, perhaps the year following, the theme would deal, primarily, with the relationship between the problems of education and the structure of society as a whole. Thus her ideas were perpetually growing and developing; it seemed as though she would never be able to say all that she had to say.

6

During this period of thirty-five years, the writer frequently had the opportunity of seeing the manner in which Dr. Montessori worked on a new problem; saw her direct the light of her intuition in turn upon the teaching of arithmetic, geometry, geography, history, biology, religion and other subjects. The process was always the same. Under the white heat of concentration, the problem broke into its component elements ("analysis of difficulties") and thereupon, easily, naturally, inevitably, a new "Montessori material" came into being, marvelously adapted to the child's nature, bearing the indelible stamp of the *Dottoressa's* genius. One got the impression that it was easy for her to create new material. Not easy, however, in the sense that it did not involve tremendous labor and concentration (for what Sir Walter Raleigh's friends said of him applied equally to the *Dottoressa* — she could "toil terribly").

In this book, which is of an introductory nature, we do not intend to say anything about Dr. Montessori's method of teaching any particular subject, except in so far as it may help to illustrate some underlying principles. We are more concerned with her principles, taken as a whole, than with any particular application of them.

THE MASTER PRINCIPLE OF THE MONTESSORI METHOD

People have often asked me, "What is the main principle of the Montessori system?" and I have often tried to find one. At first I used to think that it could conveniently be summed up as "a method of education through the senses and sense training." Then it seemed to me that "education by self-activity" described it better. Later, the phrase "education by means of liberty in a prepared environment" seemed more comprehensive. But during her later years Dr. Montessori emphasized another principle, which is, perhaps, the most fundamental of all, and one which might be looked upon as the very root and basis of her method, viz., the nature of the difference between the child and the adult.

We are all aware that children differ from adults in many ways. But what is the essential difference? The child is ignorant and the adult knows; the child is weak, the adult strong; the child lives more in the concrete, the adult in a world of ideas; the child is restless and active and must learn through activity, the adult by comparison is quiet and composed. None of these differences, according to Dr. Montessori, is fundamental; we can go deeper still and express it thus: *The child is in a state of continuous and intense transformation, of both body and mind, whereas the adult has reached the norm of the species.* Here again we have a statement expressed in biological terms. In fact, Dr. Montessori often made use of another biological term, the word *metamorphosis*, to portray the the nature of this continuously changing development which distinguishes the child from the adult. So far as the human type is concerned, the child is always in a state of becoming; the adult, on the other hand, has arrived; he has ceased to grow, because he has in fact reached the term toward which the species is aiming.

We shall now proceed to show how this principle, once clearly realized, profoundly affects our whole way of dealing with the child; how there arises from it a series of secondary principles of the highest practical value, both in the home and in the school.

THE PHYSICAL METAMORPHOSIS OF THE CHILD

As teachers, we are naturally more inclined to focus our attention on the various stages of mental development through which the child passes; yet we should never forget that the child is also passing through a bodily metamorphosis. It is quite literally a metamorphosis, for the proportions of the body of a newborn child are very different from those of the adult. It is typical of the thorough-going way Dr. Montessori did things, that, in one of her courses, she had constructed a model of a newborn child as large as an adult. When placed, side by side on the platform, next to an adult, it appeared a very monster of deformity. The creature's head was so huge that its chin came right down to the breast of the adult, and the rest of the body looked equally disproportionate.

This bodily transformation, through which the growing child has to pass before it reaches adult proportions, throws light on many of the habits of children — their imperfect equilibrium, for instance, even after they have learned to walk. This is because their heads are still too big and their feet too small by comparison with adult proportions. Who has not noticed with what delight small children walk along a line or a plank or perform some other spontaneous balancing exercise? It was, I believe, Dr. Montessori who first realized the significance of these activities, and here, as always, came to the assistance of the child's spontaneous efforts. Thus there came into being those charming exercises in balance and rhythm along a line drawn on the floor, which form a regular and attractive feature in the *casa dei bambini* (children's home). In connection, too, with this physical metamorphosis of the child we may mention the immense value of the exercises in practical life.

While it is important for us to bear in mind these physical transformations, it is even more important to remember constantly those psychic metamorphoses which succeed one another in the child's mental development.

We must now examine some of the secondary considerations which arise as corollaries from this first great fundamental principle.

THE WORK OF THE CHILD AND OF THE ADULT COMPARED

The work of the child differs profoundly from that of the adult in its nature and in its aim. The work of the adult has an external aim, to produce something outside himself — whether it is to build a bridge, till a field or formulate a code of laws. It aims at building up and transforming his environment; it is a work of conscious effort, directed to the production of an external result — in short, to help in building up a civilization.

But the work of the child is totally different. For him there does not exist this same clear consciousness of an external end to be achieved. The real aim of a child's activity is something deeper, more vital, occult — something which springs from the unconscious depths of the child's personality. This is the reason why, so often, a child does not stop when he has reached the apparent end of his labors. Supposing Tommy, aged five, goes to wash a stain off one of the little white tables in the Montessori classroom. In all probability he will not stop scrubbing when he has accomplished this aim. He will very likely go on and wash the whole surface of the table, then the legs, and perhaps even the under surface of the table. After that he may very likely turn his attention to another table, or several, which do not need washing at all.

It is true that the child started with an external aim in view, viz., to wash away the stain, but, during the process, there was born in him a mysterious passion, such as no charwoman ever knew, for washing tables. This inner urge caused him to go on working in a manner wholly uncalled for by the practical exigencies.

THE SIGNIFICANCE OF SPONTANEOUS REPETITION
IN CHILDHOOD

We are now in a position to penetrate more deeply into that well-known but rather mystifying phenomenon: the tendency of repetition which is so characteristic of small children. To give an example: a young friend of mine, aged two and a half, solemnly lifted off, and replaced, the lid of the little cylindrical box in which I keep my shaving soap no fewer than forty-two times in succession. Nobody asked him to do it in the first place, nor suggested to him to keep on doing it. At any moment during the process he was free to stop, and yet he continued as if impelled by some unseen power (which, in fact, he was).

The same thing usually happens when small children are given the Montessori cylinders. This exercise is quite simple. The child takes out all the ten cylinders from their sockets, mixes them up (they are of different sizes) and then replaces them, each in its corresponding socket. When children of about two and a half to three and a half years are presented with this material, they usually repeat it again and again, sometimes as often as twenty times in succession; and day after day, sometimes week after week — and in doing so they exhibit a concentration which is truly amazing at such an age. Here, again, it is not the mere achievement of the external end which fascinates and interests the child. If that were so he would not go on repeating it. His interest has something biological about it; it springs from that joy which always accompanies the right use of a faculty. It is even more than this: it is the joy of self-creation, the work of building the adult-to-be. By means of this constant repetition of the exercise — though, of course, the child does not realize it—he is developing an increased sensibility, a keener sensorial discrimination, and a more perfect muscular adjustment. He is also paving the way for certain important intellectual intuitions because — since with each repetition he is obliged to make a fresh comparison between the sizes of the cylinders — there is dawning ever more clearly on his mind the idea of a series of quantities, each of which varies from those above or below it by a fixed amount. Thus he is preparing his mind empirically for the idea of abstract number at a later date.

NO DIVISION OF LABOR POSSIBLE IN THE WORK OF THE CHILD

Because the work of the adult is directed toward a definite external aim, an outward result, i.e., a transformation of the environment, it follows that division of labor for him is possible and desirable. But, in the work of the child, there can be no such division of labor because his work has an internal aim. It is self-creative, directed toward the building up of the Man-That-Is-To-Be, and must therefore be done entirely by the child himself. No one can help him. Teachers and parents who think they can do this work for the child, or even a part of it, fall into an error that is responsible for much damage. As the *Dottoressa* emphatically puts it: "The child must do his own work or die." Autoeducation, or what Froebel called "self-activity," is therefore a cardinal principle in the Montessori system.

THE NONINTERVENTION OF THE TEACHER

Since the child must do his own work himself and we cannot do it for him, since real education must be in this sense self-education, there follows a principle of such vital importance that it can hardly be overemphasized. *Every useless aid we give to the child arrests his development.*

12

Every *useless* aid. This does not mean, of course, that the teacher should never help the child; it means that teacher (and parent) must guard, with unceasing vigilance, against any *unnecessary* interference with the child's work. In one sense the Montessori teacher is helping the child every moment — i.e., indirectly, in so far as she has provided for him the whole "prepared environment," which contains the means at once to stimulate and to sustain the child's creative self-activity. She must also at the proper times help the child directly, in order to initiate him into the proper use of the materials for development. Further, she must intervene to correct certain errors and to smooth away insurmountable difficulties.

In the early stages the directress will naturally be more in the foreground than she will later. At the beginning she will be more active in offering and explaining the various occupations to the children, who will, therefore, be correspondingly more passive. Little by little, however, the positions will be reversed. As the children acquire that knowledge of the exercises of practical life and of the use of the various materials, a knowledge which is the indispensable precondition of their freedom, they will begin to choose their own occupations. Thus they will be seen to proceed ever more spontaneously, and with increasing independence, along self-chosen paths — paths of ordered and progressive self-activity; while, *pari passu,* the directress becomes more passive, more of an onlooker, yet always ready to intervene in case of necessity. In this connection, Dr. Montessori often used to quote the words of St. John the Baptist, spoken in reference to the Messias: "He must increase and I must decrease."

The more successful the directress, the more completely can she retire into the background, until at length there may come moments when, from a corner of the room, she may see the whole class working away quite independently. Nothing can give her greater satisfaction than this.

It is clear that such a method differs absolutely from those that usually prevail, in which the personality of the teacher constantly dominates the scene. Dr. Montessori prefers the word *directress* to *teacher,* because her business is not so much to teach directly as to direct the child's continual supply of spontaneous mental energy into self-creative channels.

That such a method demands special training differing from that ordinarily given in the average training college goes without saying. Of the training of the Montessori directress we have already spoken elsewhere. [1]

THE CENTER AND THE PERIPHERY

Exactly what goes on in the depths of the child's soul, when he is spontaneously concentrated in this self-creative activity, none can say. The secret processes of growth on any plane, even the physical, are beyond analysis; how much more so those in the mental sphere? Happily, according to Montessori, our ignorance in this case does not greatly matter. We do not know how an apple tree grows, but it does grow and bear fruit — that is the main point. It is not necessary for the teacher, says Dr. Montessori, to delve too curiously into these mysteries which are insoluble anyhow. From the practical point of view, there is no need for her to attempt to penetrate into that inner creative center, where the intellect, will and emotions, working in conjunction with the outward and visible activity of the child, are creating the new personality.

For the directress, it is enough if she knows how to initiate the child into this outer, or peripheral, activity —

1. Maria Montessori: **Her Life and Work** by E. M. Standing. (Academy Guild Press) Chapter xviii, pp. 276 ff.

whether it be with cylinders, color tablets, number rods, grammar boxes, or any other of the materials, or with the exercises in practical life. Once this activity is set going, she can retire and let nature do the rest — confident that as long as the child continues to use the didactic materials spontaneously and with concentration, the work of self-education will keep going on, deep down in that mysterious center.

We have, then, these two aspects of the child's work: (1) an outer, motor activity at the periphery of the personality; and (2) accompanying this, a profound, invisible, creative process at the center. About this latter the teacher need not worry. It will look after itself. Her business is to feed the periphery by presenting and explaining the various occupations which are the means to development. Once she has stimulated this peripheral activity, the directress can, and should, retire, secure in the knowledge that if she interferes at this stage she will only be retarding, instead of assisting, development.

RESPECTING THE INNER RHYTHM OF THE CHILD'S LIFE

As a corollary to the difference between the nature of the child's work and that of the adult, there arises a very important practical maxim which the teacher must always bear in mind, viz., *to respect the inner rhythm of the child's soul.*

Dr. Montessori uses the term "inner rhythm" to denote the greater or less degree of mental tension which accompanies the doing of an action, i.e., a tension directed toward the fulfillment of an outside aim. It constitutes what one might call the inner tempo of the action. Or, to put it another way, one might say that this difference of inner rhythm — between that of the child and that of the adult — is the subjective aspect of that difference, already referred to, between the nature of the child's work and that of the adult.

If this description appears somewhat vague, an example will make it clear at once. Let us suppose that a child of three and a half, or four years, wishes to transport a series of objects — say the ten Montessori number rods — from the cupboard to a rug on the floor on the opposite side of the room. Quite likely the child will make ten separate journeys, going all the way there and back again ten times, each time having to thread his way carefully in and out among the little tables and chairs, and each time carrying just one rod. Ten separate journeys, one for each rod — when he could easily have done it in three or four trips. A child of that age quite commonly makes one separate journey just to carry the smallest rod, which is only four inches long. No adult would ever act in that way, nor, for that matter, would a boy of seven years or more. They would carry as many rods together as was convenient in order to save time and energy.

We adults "gnaw the nail of hurry," because our minds are stretched taut, focussed on the outward end to be achieved. We envisage the action as already accomplished in the mind's eye, and work as swiftly and economically as we can to that end. But, for the child, the doing of the action itself is the aim, albeit an unconscious one. For it is by means of the activity involved that he develops, building up and unifying his personality. This carrying of the number rods, each one separately and so carefully in and out among the other children, not hitting anyone or anything on the way, is as important for the child, at this stage, as the learning of the numbers themselves. It is important, as we shall see later, because it assists what

Montessori calls "the progressive incarnation" of the individual; that is, it helps to perfect the relationship between soul and body.

Yet even from the point of view of the child's purely mental development these ten separate journeys are not without their significance. For, to the child, each separate number rod is an entity, something to be reckoned with, and worthy of a special trip. I was observing once in a Montessori classroom when a small boy, aged four and a half, who was working with the number rods, came across the room to me, a perfect stranger, carrying one of the rods. With great seriousness he showed it to me, announcing at the same time with impressive gravity: "This — is — Seven!" After having unburdened himself of this huge discovery, he bowed, walked solemnly away, and passed out of my life for ever.

Why does the unconscionable slowness of children so often annoy us, their maddening deliberation get on our nerves? It is because we do not realize that the inner tempo of their life is so vastly different from ours. There is a "great gulf fixed" in this respect between the adult and the child, which it is our duty to bridge by an effort of our imagination — unless we happen to be mystics or Zen Buddhists. For the child and the mystic are at one in this — that they both live in a sort of eternal present. Mystic contemplation does not tend to something beyond itself; it is an end in itself. Having become "as a little child," the mystic leaves behind him the hurry and bustle of life. The reason why the slow and stately action of great liturgical ceremonies sometimes seems to us so slow and tedious is because we have not been able to project ourselves into their majestic inner rhythm, which is more of eternity than of time.

THE CHILD'S STRUGGLE FOR INDEPENDENCE

From the foregoing considerations we can see quite clearly why little children struggle so vehemently to guard their independence.

It is almost a life and death struggle for them as far as their development is concerned. Here is a little child of eighteen months who has just learned to go upstairs by herself. How she loves it! Stump, stump, stump! — always the same foot first. Such a business! Such a labor! The climbing of the pyramids is nothing to it. And what a slow process! No wonder her mother comes along, seizes the child — as the angel seized Habakkuk — and whisks her up to the top of the stairs like a sort of human elevator.

The child, of course, begins to cry; and the mother wonders why and thinks her ungrateful for the assistance she has just given her. But how grateful would an alpine climber be, if some huge giant seized him in the middle of his ascent, and planted him straight away on the summit of the Dolomite peak? Gone are all the excitement, the struggles, the glorious tension of the muscles, the sense of achievement. So, too, it is with the child. His struggle for independence is his struggle for life — for more abundant life.

Indeed the child's normal growth may be regarded as a series of steps toward more and more complete independence. Birth is the first of these. Then, when the child is weaned, he takes another step. Yet another comes when he learns to speak, before which time he was dependent on others to interpret his wants. When the child learns to walk, he passes another milestone in the same direction — always toward more complete independence.

In the home and the school, therefore, the adult must learn to respect the child's strivings after independence. It is often much easier, and much quicker, for the parent or teacher to do things instead of letting the children do them. Take dressing and undressing, for instance. Yet, for the child's own sake, the mother must learn to have greater patience. I was once tutor in the house of an Italian nobleman where there were two big boys of twelve and thirteen years of age who had not even learned to brush their own hair. It was always done for them by their mother or the governess. Small wonder these boys were spoilt and undisciplined almost beyond belief!

In passing, we might point out that this independence of the child — for which Dr. Montessori so strenuously fights — has nothing to do with any theories of political or religious independence; nor does it in any way violate the principle of necessary obedience to all rightly constituted authority. Rather, the kind of independence to which she refers is a biological necessity. According to this point of view, to become independent in any sphere means to be able to do for yourself what hitherto someone had to do for you.

THE NECESSITY OF LIBERTY IN EDUCATION

We have already noted that the child displays a remarkable tendency to repeat certain actions over and over again. Once shown how to use a piece of the didactic material, for instance, he will go on repeating the exercise many times and on many different days. We have noted, also, that this peripheral activity is the exterior sign of a corresponding inner development at the center, a ripening of the mental faculties. We can now realize why it is so important that the child should be free to work at any occupation, without the teacher's interference, for as long as he wishes to do so. The child must be free to repeat the exercise as many times as he wants, because in this matter of the inner ripening, he himself must be the final judge. Instinctively he knows when the process is complete, just as a normal person knows when he has eaten enough.

When this inner ripening has taken place, the almost furious concentration of the child on the occupation becomes relaxed and his interest subsides. By these and other signs, the child shows that he is ready to pass on to the next stage. This is the psychological moment for the directress to step in and point out the next part of the way. Sometimes, as we shall see, the child finds the next stage unassisted, through a sudden and spontaneous expansion of his mental horizon.

MONTESSORI EXPLOSIONS

During this prolonged activity with the material (inner and outer activity at the same time), the child is preparing himself for the next stage in his mental metamorphosis, which sometimes he reaches with surprising suddenness. The long, tranquil, joyful work with the material, and the profound persuasion that comes with it, often bring about a spontaneous leap of the mind to a new and higher level. At these moments, just because it is working at its own pace and according to its own laws, the intellect of the child discovers in a flash some new law or relationship arising out of what it has previously been doing. These sudden revelations fill the child's soul with an exquisite joy which is beautiful to behold. They call to mind Emerson's phrase: "Generalization is an influx of divinity into the mind; hence the thrill that attends." These "Montessori explosions" form one of the most fascinating and characteristic features of the Montessori schoolroom.

It is interesting to notice that, in the realm of biology, there are analogous "saltations." (Cf. de Vries, the Dutch biologist.) Take the well-known example of the chrysalis stage in the development of the butterfly. When the caterpillar spins his cocoon and remains motionless without taking any food for weeks at a time, it looks as though no further growth is taking place. Yet, if one examines carefully, one can see that, beneath the skin of the chrysalis, new organs—wings, legs, eyes, mouth parts, etc.— are already forming. When this inner development is complete and the butterfly emerges, we see what appears to be a sudden change. But in reality it is only the visible result of an accumulation of inner changes. In the same way, a casual observer might imagine that the child was wasting time, thus repeating the same or similar exercises with the material for such a long time without taking in any fresh mental food. But in reality all this time there is taking place, deep in the child's mind at the center, an accumulation of experience upon which the intellect is working in its own way and at its own pace. The human intellect, working spontaneously according to its own laws, tends, by its very nature, to rise above, dominate, set in order and classify, all those experiences which are brought to it through the avenues of the senses.

The great value of the Montessori material is that it presents the nature of the outside world to the child in such an orderly way that it assists his intellect (which is the principle of order in the mind) to recognize, in flashes of intuition, the order in the world outside, thereby making it a part of itself. The order of the macrocosm is thus reflected in the microcosm.

This method of growth, by sudden mental expansions, is paralleled by the laws of life on other planes. The post-Darwinian researches of de Vries, Bateman and others indicate that even the progress of the species as a whole is not a continuous one, but proceeds by sudden mutations.

THE IMMENSE SPONTANEOUS ACTIVITY
OF THE CHILD'S INTELLECT

These Montessori explosions bear striking witness to the spontaneous activity of the child's intellect. Speaking generally, we may say that Dr. Montessori's system is based on belief in the spontaneous working of the human intellect. The older methods of education assumed that it was not natural for children to work at their lessons without being spurred on by rewards or punishments. It was a chief part of the teacher's work to whip up their flagging spirits and to keep their little noses to the grindstone.

Dr. Montessori's idea is quite different. If children at school do not show a disposition to work spontaneously, then the fault lies not with the children but with the teacher and her manner of presenting the subjects. If children are bored, uninterested and uncomprehending, it is because, in the method of teaching, there are obstacles which prevent the child's intellect from functioning as it ought. In fact, in Aristotelian philosophy it is a fundamental principle that a faculty *must* work, all hindrances being removed. This is, indeed, the very proof of the existence of any faculty.

It is as natural for the intellect to function spontaneously as it is for the heart to beat. It is as natural for the baby to begin making comparisons, classifications, and judgments as it is for him to learn to stand and walk.

The statement that the child's intellect is sufficient — through its own *spontaneous* activity — to drive him on to acquire the elements of culture may seem to many teachers absurd on the face of it. Yet, if one pauses to reflect on the work which has already been done by the child's intellect by the time he reaches the age of three, i.e, before he goes even to a kindergarten, then indeed it does not seem such an unreasonable assertion.

But it requires a serious effort of imaginative thinking before the adult can realize with any clearness the astonishing amount of mental work which is accomplished by the very small child, even before he can speak.

Consider for a moment the gigantic task which confronts the newborn infant. He finds himself weak and helpless in a new world, a world so new that the infant is unknown even to himself. He has no ideas of space or time, of color or form, of cause or effect. He has, in fact, no ideas of any kind, for ideas have to be built up from sensory experience, and of this he has had none. He has no memory, and there is, therefore, nothing in the world around him which he can recognize. As Professor William James well said, to the newborn infant "the universe is nothing but a big, buzzing, booming confusion."

Out of this bewildering chaos of impressions which pour in upon him through every sense, the tiny mite has to build up an orderly world, a cosmos; in fact, one might say two worlds, one within and one without. Almost from the day of his birth, he must set to work to learn the significance of the things in his environment, their purposes, their causes, their relationships. He must compare, contrast, classify unceasingly. He must learn, for instance, through repeated experiences and his own experiments, the spatial relationship of things — that some are near and others far off. He must learn to distinguish between the present, the past and the future; between the self and the not-self; between experience in reality and experience in dreams. His little mind must grapple with the problem of persons and animals around him; their comings and goings, their aims, their interrelations. Even the functions of his own bodily organs are unknown to him and there is a world of discovery in this alone.

Then, too, he must learn the difference between things real and things imaginary—a task often made unnecessarily difficult for him by the well-meaning stupidity of adults. (This, by the way, is the basis of Dr. Montessori's much misunderstood criticism of fairy tales.)

And, as if this were not a large enough task for this small creature setting out on life's journey, he has to work under a handicap unknown to the adult, which we may describe as "the difficulty of the instrument." The newborn child, says Dr. Montessori, is "imperfectly incarnated." Hence we have the tragedy of a being who is intelligently wide-awake, and as yet has no means of expressing himself clearly. The infant possesses a soul which has to create for itself its own instrument for expression. (We may note in passing that it is partly because he *is* "imperfectly incarnated" that the child learns best to the accompaniment of an external activity. He instinctively acts in this manner because it tends to perfect the relationship between his soul and body.) But to return to the mental task which confronts the small child. He has also to struggle with the mysteries of human speech and the practical acquisition of a language.

That the small child, after measuring himself against all these colossal tasks, comes out of the ordeal fresh and smiling and eager for more is, could we see it in the right light, the clearest proof of the extraordinary spontaneous power of the human intellect. The Montessori method, we repeat, bases itself on belief in this spontaneous activity of the child's intellect. It sets to work on the supposition, verified times without number, that this infantile intellect—which has already accomplished such prodigies in the first three years of the child's life—will not cease to work spontaneously when the same child enters the Montessori infants' school.

THE YOUNG EXPLORER

Every child is a born explorer. From the first moment he opens his eyes, they are wide with wonder. The world is full of mysteries on every side. Things which are commonplace to us fill him with an ecstasy of surprise and fascination. The child is like a savage, brought suddenly into a civilized country—where at every turn he sees strange objects and customs and is ignorant of their names, their uses and their relationships.

This is a point which cannot be too strongly emphasized. It is only by a real effort of the imagination that we can get any idea of the way a small child looks on life. Let an adult visit some huge factory full of strange, whirling, mechanical devices, almost human in their ingenuity, yet incomprehensible in their manner of working, and often in their scope too. Let him feel the bewildering strangeness of it all and at the same time its intriguing fascination, and he will get a faint notion of what our everyday environment must seem like to the small children who have not yet grown up into the "light of common day."

The ordinary things of life are so full of wonder to them that they cannot understand the meaning of the *extra*-ordinary. Let a conjuror produce a rabbit out of a top hat and the child of two is in no way surprised by this feat. For all he knows, such may be the natural habitat of the animal. On the other hand, this beautiful, new, furry creature with the long ears and wobbly nose is to him a real wonder far surpassing the conjuror's skill, of which he is not even aware. G. K. Chesterton observes that the sentence: "He opened the door" is sufficient for the child of two. To open and shut the door is, in fact, for him a new

25

and joyful accomplishment; indeed he may do it ten or twenty times in succession just for the fun of it.

Watch carefully any child of two or three years of age, and you will see that he is incessantly engaged in exploring, experimenting, discovering. Everything is of interest to him—a piece of stick that floats on the water, the water itself (surely one of God's masterpieces), a stone that sinks, a passing water cart, a piece of colored paper—all is grist to his mill. Touching, handling, moving, rearranging, dissecting, opening, shutting, collecting, comparing, these little scientists are incessantly prying into everything *"as if they were God's spies."* (*King Lear*). To them every passage is a secret passage, every walk a voyage of discovery, every day

> "is an arch wherethrough gleams that untraveled
> Land, whose margin fades for ever and for ever
> As they move."

Indeed this sense of wonder is one of the most attractive features of childhood, and happy is he who never loses it, for, "wondering, he shall reach the Kingdom."

This spirit of exploration, this unceasing quest for experience is not to be confused with a squirrel-like curiosity. It is not idle curiosity that prompts the child to break open a toy to see "what makes the wheels go round." Rather it is the profound urge of the human intellect seeking for causes, for what Froebel described as "inner connections." It is the human intellect working because it must, because it *is*; it is the spirit of man going forth undaunted to unlock the secrets of the universe. Well, indeed, did Wordsworth apostrophize the small child as

> "thou whose exterior semblance
> doth belie thy soul's immensity."

But let us leave the poets and come back to the practical

bearing of all this in the classroom. It is not to be supposed that the character of the child changes as he walks across the street from his home to the kindergarten. How is it, then, that this same child, so filled with a zest for new knowledge, who wears out his parents at home asking a thousand questions a day, becomes so dull, listless and apathetic when placed in the serried ranks of the ordinary nursery school? It is not that the spirit of discovery has left him (as though it were a divine afflatus that comes and goes); it is simply that, in the old-fashioned school with old-fashioned methods, he has no chance to make discoveries for himself.

In the first place, the teacher is doing all the discovery, in so far as there is any, for him. There is nothing more annoying than to go for a walk and have some officious person busily pointing out the things one would much rather see and find out for oneself, at one's own pace, and in one's own way.

In the second place, the child cannot set about making discoveries because he is tied down, both physically and mentally. Physically, because he must remain sitting still in his appointed place; and mentally, because the teacher has chosen the way, is setting the pace, and is continually prodding the child's attention on from one thing to another. Under those circumstances the spirit of discovery, or the spontaneous activity of the child's intellect, has no chance to reveal itself.

What Montessori says, in effect, is this: "Arrange the child's life in such a way as to give this spirit of inquiry full play in the schoolroom, and you will see it express itself in the most marvelous manner." The directress must be there, of course, to guide the children on to, and along the paths of, discovery. For it is one thing to have someone stimulate your interest and point out the way so that

you can walk in it alone, and quite another to have someone always with you directing your every footstep, your
every glance, and even your every thought.

Suppose there is a man with a great instinctive urge to
explore some out-of-the-way part of the world. Let him
attend a lecture on the African jungle by a returned explorer and he may be fired with a great desire to go there
himself. Such is the function of the Montessori teacher:
to stimulate interest, and thus send the child off on what
are to him new paths of discovery. This is much more
interesting than always listening to the teacher. How
would the African explorer like to be condemned to listen
perpetually to someone else relating his experiences,
instead of getting away into the jungle to blaze a new trail
for himself?

THE EXPLORER'S PARADISE

When the child comes into the prepared environment of
the Montessori school, he finds himself in a place from
which fascinating paths for exploration lead out in all
directions. And he finds in the teacher a willing guide
who explains the different routes and prepares him with
just enough instruction and materials (*and no more*) to
enable him to set off by himself. What these various
routes are, and how to present the child with the necessary
information to enable him to travel them alone, forms a
large part of the special training of the Montessori
directress. It is important that the teacher should give the
child sufficient information to stimulate his interest and
enable him to use the material; but at the same time it is
equally important that she give only the *necessary minimum,* so that there remains the maximum field for the
child's own individual research. All this is only another

way of saying that the Montessori method is one of auto-education.

The real discoverer is not one who wanders aimlessly through an unknown land, seeing new places and gaining new impressions, only to let each successive experience efface the memory of previous ones as wave follows wave to be lost in the sea. On the contrary, great discoverers are men who *systematically* collect information, who scientifically record and classify their experiences—men who are always striving to make the new fit on to the old, the unknown to the known. If such an explorer comes across a new river, for instance, he at once begins to ask himself where is its source? Whither does it go? Is it a tributary of some river already known? In a word, he sorts out and classifies all the experiences that come to him on his journey, placing them in appropriate pigeonholes, thus building up a correlated system of knowledge. And the more pigeonholes he has in his mind, the greater will be his value as an explorer. The more order he brings in his mind to the undiscovered country, the more knowledge he will take away from it.

So, too, with the little explorer in the Montessori school. He is not permitted to wander aimlessly about, now here, now there, gleaning fitful and inconsequent impressions as whim or curiosity may direct. This is the reason no child is allowed to occupy himself with any portion of the didactic material until he has been fully instructed in its proper use, for the *correct* use of the material forms the path which leads from the known to the unknown. Of what value would be a theodolite or a barometer or a magnetic compass to an explorer who did not know their uses?

We touch here upon a point which is often misunderstood in relation to the Montessori method — one which occasions much mis-directed criticism. People often say: "What purpose can be served by giving such small children all these carefully and scientifically prepared sensorial materials — these color tablets, rods, cylinders, cubes, prisms, and what not? Does not the child see all these colors—and more—around him every hour, and every hour of the day? Does he not see all sorts of geometrical forms—rectangular, cylindrical, circular, etc.—in his home environment, and of varying sizes, too? Is he not constantly touching and feeling, manipulating things wherever he is? Why then all this unnecessary and complicated material—unnecessary, because it does not give him any new sensations; and complicated because it must be made with scientific accuracy? And anyhow, what is the use of wasting all this scientific accuracy (not to mention the expense) upon children who are so undeveloped that they cannot even count?"

The answer to these objections is that the main purpose of the Montessori material—especially the sensory material—*is not so much to give the child new impressions as to give order to the impressions already received.*

True knowledge consists, not in the awareness of isolated facts, but in ordered systems of related facts. It cannot be denied that a part of the business of education should consist in supplying the child with necessary information. But this forms only what one might call the raw material of culture. It is the least essential part. Real education comes only when the intellect rises above and dominates the information it has received. The mere facts presented are like iron filings lying in disorder on a piece of paper. The intellect is like the invisible magnet underneath, which, by its compelling power, works out and systematizes the unrelated raw material of experience into an organized system of thought.

THE PSYCHOLOGY OF THE CYLINDERS

This point is so often misunderstood and is so important in its bearing on the Montessori method that it is worth while lingering a little longer over it. Let us take as an example a set of the Montessori cylinders already referred to. This is a material which has been often criticized (but only by those who have never seen it in use) as artificial and unadapted to the needs of small children. One set consists of ten cylinders, which vary accurately in height from the smallest, which is five centimenters, to the tallest which is ten centimeters. Each cylinder fits exactly into a corresponding socket in a wooden block. The exercise is quite simple; it consists in removing all the cylinders (holding each by the little knob at the top), mixing them up, and then returning each to its appropriate socket.

Whatever the reason may be, the fascination which this exercise has for a child of about three and a half is quite astonishing. I once gave a set as a birthday present to a little girl on her third birthday. She played with them all afternoon, and actually took them to bed with her, lying in her cot with the block of cylinders (hard bedfellow) on one side, and her Teddy-bear on the other. It was by means of this same material that Dr. Montessori first realized the profound possibilities of concentration latent in the small child. (See *The Secret of Childhood*, pp. 133-5).

Wherein lies the fascination and the educative value of this material? First of all, the mere taking of something out of its socket—like the stopper out of a bottle—and returning it again, is always a fascinating exercise for a small child, because it is a training in muscular adjustment. Then again, at this stage—when the child is passing through a sensitive period for order—the mere putting an object back in its place is, in itself, a cause of satisfaction. But without doubt the greatest value, and the greatest attraction, of the cylinders lies in that scientific accuracy which so many critics deplore as unsuited and pedantic. For it is this accurate grading, this regular and constant variation, which gives to the dawning intelligence of the child such excellent material to work on. It presents, in fact, the basis for attaining to various intellectual intuitions. Thus there arises, at first very dimly, and then more clearly, in the child's mind as he repeats this exercise *the abstract notion of a regular series of objects varying in height*—a notion, which, as we have already mentioned, is similar to that which lies at the root of the idea of number.

Of course, it cannot be denied that there are many other objects besides the cylinders of varying heights in the child's ordinary environment. There are, for instance, people of varying heights, from tall grownups to small babies. But, and here is the vital point, the child does not see ten persons going down the street, one behind the other, all in a line, and each varying in height from the one in front and behind by a fixed and constant amount. If he did, it must be granted, it would seem a sufficiently arresting sight; but even then the child would not have the opportunity of manipulating the members of this unique family himself for hours at a time—arranging and comparing them, day after day, as he does with the cylinders, until the abstract idea of *gradation* comes like the morning light, imperceptibly and without effort, and illumines his intelligence.

The same sort of thing happens with the color tablets, whose aim is to show gradations of the same color. Almost certainly the child has seen all these different shades before, at different times in his brief life; but *it is the seeing of them all together, and in the order of their regular gradation, which gives them new significance in his eyes.* For it is precisely this which brings into mental focus the very notion of gradation in colors. And is is not simply a question of seeing this gradation; but also what one might call *doing* it—that is, of repeating many times—the manipulative exercise itself first mixing up the various shades, and then putting them out again in their proper order.

KEYS TO THE UNIVERSE

These carefully graded sensory materials, when properly used, set in order the child's past experiences; and, like keys to the universe, unlock fresh treasures in the environment. Thus a child of four, who had been working with the graded color tablets, said to a lady visitor as soon as she came into the room: "Your dress is exactly the same shade of blue as a flower in the next room!" And so it was. In a class I was visiting a small boy came up to me and informed me with great solemnity that my coat was brown. A Cardinal, visiting a Montessori school in Italy, presented the children with a bag of biscuits. Now it happened that these biscuits were made in various geometric shapes. To the Cardinal's astonishment, the children did not eat the biscuits in their joy at being able to recognize the geometric forms whose acquaintance they had recently made in working through the "geometric cabinet" — a material for sensorial geometry. In another Italian school, a lady visitor (of no great discernment) complained to the directress of the bad manners of some of the children because one or two of the tiny tots had come to her and fingered her dress. She did not realize that the little ones had merely been delicately touching the surface of the dress to discover its texture. Only that morning these same children had been busy with the box of fabrics. This is an exercise of touch, which they do blindfolded, the aim of which is to explore and compare, through the tactile sense, a series of cloths of various textures from a rough hempen homespun to the finest silk. As a consequence of their morning's experience, they were going around testing, by feel and touch, the texture of any woven materials they could find—including the visitor's dress.

In every *casa dei bambini* it happens quite naturally that children who have been learning numbers with the number rods and spindles, etc., begin spontaneously to count any group of objects in their environment which can be thought of as a numerical series. On one occasion I was observing in a Montessori class in Acton, London, with about fifteen other visitors. I was amused to see one small child of about five years standing in the middle of the room, quietly counting the visitors to herself. Instead of being embarrassed by so many strangers, she was simply regarding them as another set of similar objects on which she could test her newly acquired ability to count.

CORRECT USE OF MATERIALS ESSENTIAL

Some critics, especially the Froebelians, are up in arms against the Montessori system because the child is not allowed to use the didactic materials in any way that happens to take his fancy. If the child, for instance, instead of using the color tablets for matching or grading begins to build a house with them, they think he should be allowed to do so. And when the directress tactfully turns the child's attention back to the scope of the material, or presents him with another occupation, they think it an unwarrantable interference with the child's liberty. The Froebelians, as we have noted more fully elsewhere, think that the child should be encouraged "to make everything out of everything."

From what we have said with regard to the principle of order in the materials, which helps to bring more order in the child's mind, we can clearly see the reason Dr. Montessori always insists upon their right use. It is, in fact, only another way of saying that the child must respect the principle of order which is inherent in each of the materials. By so doing, the principle of order in the child—which is the intellect—is strengthened. The more powerful an intellect, the more surely does it act like a light which illuminates and puts in order, making clear what was hitherto chaotic and unrelated. Thus, unless the child had used the color tablets properly—i.e., to set the colors in order in a chromatic scale—she would not have been led to see spontaneously the exact similarity of shade between the lady's dress and the flower in the next room. Unless he had used the geometric material for the purpose for which it was intended, that boy, walking along the Pincio gardens with Dr. Montessori, would never have exclaimed: "Just look how the works of man are all made up of squares and circles and triangles and so on!"

ORDER ESSENTIAL IN THE PREPARED ENVIRONMENT

In training her teachers Dr. Montessori insists again and again, not only on the right use of the material, but also on the teacher's seeing to it that the whole environment of the child in the Montessori school be kept scrupulously in order, with a place for everything and everything in its place. For it is from this order which he finds around him that the dawning order in the child's mind is strengthened. Both for teacher and for scholars, in the Montessori schoolroom, there could not be a more appropriate motto than that of St. Augustine: "Serve order and order will serve you."

After reading what we have written concerning the place of the intellect in the Montessori school, some readers might get the impression that Dr. Montessori lays too great an emphasis on intellectual development, an emphasis which might prove harmful to small children and lead to a forced and one-sided development. That this fear is quite unfounded will become evident as we consider the next aspect of our subject.

SENSITIVE PERIODS IN THE CHILD'S DEVELOPMENT

At the beginning of this book, we took as the most fundamental principle underlying the Montessori system the recognition of the fact that "the child is in a state of continuous and intense transformation, whereas the adult has reached the norm of the species." We have already seen how this applies to the child's physical growth. We have also pointed out how it affects the nature of the child's "work" when compared with that of the adult. We have now to consider more carefully how this continual transformation, or metamorphosis, is revealed, during the child's mental growth, in what Dr. Montessori calls the law of sensitive periods.

The term "sensitive period" is taken from the sphere of biology and was coined by the famous Dutch biologist, Hugo de Vries, to describe the results of his researches in in the development of certain organisms. Put briefly, the law of sensitive periods amounts to the recognition of the fact that "certain determinating conditions in the environment are able to bring about different results, according as to whether they are applied at different stages in the individual's development."

To make this more clear, let us take an example. There

is a certain butterfly (*Porthesia*) which lays its eggs upon the bark of a tree. When the young caterpillars emerge from the eggs, they have a special sensibility to light and move towards it. As a consequence these tiny creatures make their way towards the tips of the branches where the light is strongest. There they find the youngest leaves, which are most suited to their tender mouth-parts. After a while, however, these caterpillars, now grown larger, lose this special sensitivity to light, and so make their way indifferently to all parts of the tree. At this stage it is a good thing for them to do this, as their mouths are now strong enough for them to nourish themselves on the larger and stronger leaves. It is interesting to note that the disappearance of this sensitive period, which has served its purpose, is as important for the insect's development as was its presence in the earlier stage. For, as Montessori says, "conditions which are extremely favorable to development during a certain stage may become ineffectual, or even unfavorable, during a later period."

In a similar way, as the child passes through various stages of development, he reveals certain sensitive periods, during which he shows "aptitudes and possibilities in the psychical order" which afterwards disappear. When the child is passing through such a sensitive period, he will attach himself to certain exercises, activities, or occupations with an interest and a concentration he can never again display for that particular kind of work. At such times he will accomplish, quite spontaneously, labors of patience and industry which are truly astonishing; which upset, in fact, all our previous notions of fatigue in respect to learning.

"When the child does exercises which correspond to the needs of his 'present sensibility' he advances and reaches a degree of perfection which is inimitable in other moments of life; and, even without fatigue, increases his own strength, thereby proving the joy which comes with the satisfying of a real need of life." For, strangely enough, the child is not worn out by these Herculean labors. On the contrary, he seems refreshed and stronger for them, as though they had fortified his mind—indeed his whole personality—with some invisible nourishment.

From an educational point of view these sensitive periods are of immense importance and it is the business of the teacher to recognize, use and serve them. Since in each of them the child shows a special sensibility to certain impressions and actions (the outward evidence of an inner need), it becomes our duty to see that he finds in his environment that which will supply and satisfy it.

THE SENSITIVE PERIOD FOR LANGUAGE

Generally speaking, the Montessori didactic materials have been created to correspond to these sensitive periods and to supply their needs.

One of the most remarkable of the sensitive periods, one which reveals itself in the child's early years, is a special susceptibility to hearing and reproducing the sounds of spoken language. So great is the child's capacity for words at this stage that he can pick up two or three languages at the same time without any special effort. Never again will he be able to learn the pronunciation of a language so perfectly nor with such ease. It would seem that children have such a void within them, waiting to be filled with words, that, at this stage, they sometimes make up an extra nonsense language of their own to satisfy it.

Nor is this special suspectibility to hearing and reproducing sounds confined to words. A young friend of mine (aged two) casually remarked to me one day as he passed me in the garden: "It says oo-era! oo-era!" I was somewhat mystified at first, but a little investigation revealed that he was referring to the wheel of his little wheelbarrow, which, as it revolved, made an almost imperceptible noise. This he had observed and reproduced with striking accuracy.

A practical application of this sensitive period is, if possible, to expose children at this stage to hearing a foreign tongue, so that they may learn an extra language—almost without noticing it.

"WORDS, WORDS, WORDS"

Later on, from about five to six and a half years, there comes a somewhat similar stage when the child displays the same sort of interest in *written* words. If you were to ask him, during *this* sensitive period, what he was studying, the child might suitably reply as Hamlet said to Polonius: "Words, words, words." The mystery of the written word has just been revealed to his understanding and for the time being the wonder of it absorbs him completely. The single word by itself suffices at this period, without the added interest formed by the synthesis of a number of words to make a sentence. As Montessori says: "The little child feels a great joy in discovering: 'How wonderful it is that just the little letter "Z" can make all the difference between me (*io*) and my uncle (*Zio*)!'"

Still later there comes another sensitive period in connection with language. This is *par excellence* the time to learn grammar, for now the child is fascinated by the study of different kinds of words and of their relations to each other in forming sentences. Looking back on his own schooldays and the way in which he learned grammar, the reader may be inclined to think this an exaggeration. Nevertheless, it is quite true that grammar is one of the most popular subjects in the Montessori school. In fact Dr. Montessori goes so far as to say that, even if there were no practical advantages to be derived from the study of grammar (as of course there are), we should still *have* to give it to the child, at this stage, in response to his need for it as a necessary and satisfying mental gymnastic.

"DROPPED STITCHES" IN MENTAL DEVELOPMENT

The importance to the teacher of these sensitive periods cannot be overestimated because, in each of them, the child can learn some particular thing better and with less fatigue than at any other time. Indeed, if one may commit the crime of adapting Shakespeare a little, one might say:

"There is a tide in the affairs of *children*
Which, taken at the flood, leads on to fortune;
Omitted, all the voyage of their lives
Is spent in shallows and in miseries."

Perhaps "shallows and miseries" is too strong a term to describe the effect of neglecting to make use of these sensitive periods because, even if we do not "take them at the flood," the child will still grow up and become a man. Nevertheless his inner development will not be so full and harmonious as it might have been. If, while you are knitting a sweater, you drop some stitches, you can still go on and finish the garment; but it will not be so complete and perfect as if you had not dropped those stitches on the way. Similarly, in the mental and social development of most of us, there have been "dropped stitches" of which we are sometimes only too well aware. It is true that we *have* grown up in spite of it; yet we feel that our personalities would have been fuller and more harmonious if each expanding faculty had been given its fullest scope in the time of its particular sensitive period.

How many persons have a shocking caligraphy, simply because they did not have the opportunity of learning to write at the time when they had a sensitive period for touching forms? Montessori children learn to write at the age of four and a half or five by touching around the forms of the sandpaper letters. That is the proper age to learn to write—on the tide of the sensitive period for touch—and a child will learn better, more easily and more quickly than at any subsequent age. How many people grow up awkward in their movements, because, at the time when the whole bent of their nature was toward such activities as the exercises in practical life, they were not introduced to them? Again, think of the number of unfortunate people who pronounce their own language badly, simply because, when they were at the sensitive period for picking up words, their parents and teachers did not take enough care to protect them from an imperfect lingual environment, or, at least, try to correct their errors at that time. Most grown-ups feel that they could have realized a fuller artistic or musical development, as to both execution and appreciation, if only they had been given the opportunity at the period when these aspirations were most strong in them.

Perhaps the most tragic of all "lost" sensitive periods are those which may occur in the religious development of children. The soul of the child is especially sensitive to religious influences. As Dr. Montessori says: "Little children, because of their innocence, can feel in a purer and more intense manner, even if less definitely than the adult, the need of God's presence. Their souls seem to be more open to divine intuitions than the adult's, in spite of the latter's more perfectly developed intelligence and skill in reasoning." Yet, in spite of the possession of this special sensibility, it happens all too frequently in our times that a parent will say: "I have no definite religion myself and I do not intend to force one on my child. He can choose for himself when he is grown up." Such an attitude is about as reasonable as if one were to say: "I do not know what my child's favorite dish will be when he is grown up. And so, in the meanwhile, I shall not give him any food at all."

THE SENSITIVE PERIOD FOR ORDER

One of the most interesting sensitive periods, through which all children pass, is that which Dr. Montessori describes as the sensitive period for order. The *Dottoressa* was, I believe, the first to draw attention to this fascinating and rather mysterious phenomenon. But, like the continent of America, once discovered, it can easily be verified —in this case by anyone in daily contact with very young children.

This sensitive period for order begins to reveal itself very strongly as the child reaches his second year and lasts for about two years, being most marked in the third year.

During all this period the child displays an almost passionate interest in the order of things in both time and space. It seems to him, at this stage, a particularly vital matter that everything in his environment should be kept in its accustomed place; and similarly that all the actions of the day should be carried out in their accustomed routine. In fact, he becomes a positive ritualist in such matters.

Thus, if the corner of a rug be turned up, or an ornament out of its usual place, or a coat left on a chair when it ought to be on its hook, or the lid of a box left lying nearby instead of on it, you will generally find that it is the small child of two and a half who is distressed by these irregularities, rather than his older brother or sister of eight or twelve years.

It is quite astonishing to what a degree children at this stage can be distressed by what they consider an interference with the proper position of things in their environment, or with the order in which they should be carried out. In fact, children may become so upset from this that they may fall into fits of crying, almost into convulsions. Often the person in charge, who has no idea of the real cause, imagines it to be only "another of the child's wilful fits of temper." (For other examples, illustrating this sensitive period for order, see Montessori's *The Secret of Childhood,* Chapter III, also page 135).

It is typical of Dr. Montessori's genius that she has not only observed this phenomenon in small children, but has also divined the psychological cause of it. (See *Maria Montessori: Her Life and Work,* Chapter VII.)

THE PREPARED ENVIRONMENT AND
THE SENSITIVE PERIOD FOR ORDER

For the moment, it is sufficient to point out that this sensitive period for order has its very practical aspects. It would be manifestly impossible to permit some thirty to forty small children to move about freely in the same room, letting them choose their occupations at will, if it were necessary to impose this sense of order from without. It is just because this feeling for order is already so strongly present in the child at this age that it is a practical possibility to give so much freedom, even to tiny tots, as is done in the Montessori infant school. For these children find, in the general arrangement of the Montessori classroom and the manner of life in it, just that kind of environment for which they instinctively crave—i.e., an environment where everything has its proper place, and where there is an exact, almost ritualistic, manner of carrying out every action. Thus, suppose a child decides to occupy himself with the Pink Tower. He finds a precise and definite series of actions waiting to be carried out. First, he must put back in its proper place the material he has been using previously. Then he must go to another part of the room where he will find some small colored rugs which are used to spread on the floor. Having chosen the color he prefers, he must now take the rug and spread it on a suitable spot. Next, he goes to another definitely known and constant place where the Pink Tower blocks are always kept. Having transported the blocks, one by one, to the rug, he may now begin to build the tower. Even this he can do successfully only by choosing the blocks in a certain order. After occupying himself with the blocks for as long as he likes, he must then return them to their proper place. Next, the rug must be folded, also in a precise and definite manner, and returned to its place. And similarly with any other materials he may happen to choose.

As we noted above, finding things in their proper places, and putting them back again, gives the child a special delight at this stage, just because it satisfies this sensitive period for order. If we respond to his need, at this time and in this way, he can be carried on the crest of the wave of this special susceptibility into the formation of habits of order, which could never at any later period be so easily established.

To judge by the reactions of children during this epoch, it would seem as though the positions of the objects in the rooms in which they are accustomed to live are, as it were, photographed on their minds—and this without any effort. One day, after I had been lecturing on the subject, a teacher related a rather amusing experience in confirmation of this trait. A short time previously, she had exchanged the positions of two cards hanging on the wall in her Montessori infant class, one being a grammar card and the other a piece of poetry. "Next morning," she said, "the very first child who came into the room noticed the change. At once, without saying a word—as if it were merely a matter of choice, not to say duty—the little girl changed the two cards back to their former positions. The day following the same thing occurred, only it happened to be another child this time. Several days more in succession I changed the cards, and every time one child or another would observe the change and rectify it. It evidently gave the children such a keen feeling of dissatisfaction not to find these objects in their usual places that they felt an inner need to re-establish the accustomed order." "After about four or five days," continued the teacher, "I gave up struggling against the current and let them have their own way, for it was not a matter of real importance. I was surprised at their pertinacity, for at that time I did not understand the reason for it."

As Dr. Montessori points out, there is, however, a limit to the capacity which the child has, at this epoch, for mentally photographing the position of the objects in his environment; and this limit has an important bearing on the size of the environment which we should prepare for the child and on the number of children in it. A room with about forty children should be the limit—after that the little individual feels that he is lost in the crowd.

THE IMPORTANCE OF MAKING USE
OF SENSITIVE PERIODS

When we consider education, as a whole, in the light of these sensitive periods, and adapt ourselves to them, it is truly surprising to what a rich mental and moral development children attain naturally and without effort—and at a very early age. The perfection of the sensorial development of the child in the Montessori schools, their graceful precision of movement, their exquisite handwriting, their appreciation of good music, their sense of harmony in colors as revealed in their spontaneous designs, the originality and freshness of their compositions, their self-discipline, their serene and joyous social demeanor, the simple

45

yet profound expression of their religious sentiment—all these qualities, and many others, continually astonish visitors on account of the tender years of the children who so charmingly display them. Yet it is just because the children *are* so young that it has been possible for them to acquire these perfections; for they have been able to profit by the various occupations specially created to utilize for cultural purposes these powerful sensitive periods through which they are passing,

THE AGE OF SENSATION

Many of these sensitive periods overlap, because some last longer than others, but we do not have space here to go into detail on this point. We must not leave the subject, however, without reference to another sensitive period— one of the longest and most important. It lasts, in fact, with varying degrees of intensity, from birth to the age of six or thereabouts. We refer to the well-known interest which all children display in the sensorial qualities of objects—color, form, dimension, surface, weight, sound, movement, and so on.

Every mother knows how tiny children love to touch and handle things, to move them about, examine them, finger them, stroke them, shake them, and, if possible, pull them to pieces. Their little hands are never idle; they are constantly "meddling with something or other." How often, indeed, does this trait get those "young explorers" into trouble, eliciting from the adult world such an outcry as: "Don't touch that vase, Tommy, you'll break it!" Yet, in spite of such warnings, in spite sometimes of even severe punishments, the tiny hands insist on touching, feeling, exploring, all the livelong day—as though in obedience to some imperious instinct which no adult discipline can subdue.

Look at any baby and you will see that he always has something in his fingers. It may be a piece of paper which he turns over and over with all the seriousness of a professor examining a new specimen. It *is* a new specimen to him. If the stroller stops for a moment outside a shop window, the baby is up at once—as far as his straps allow—and starts feeling the glass or whatever else comes within reach of those tentacles of his opening mind . . . his fingers. He never loses a minute, but takes every new opportunity of investigating the world.

Watch the same child, two or three years later, playing by himself, and you will always find that he (or she) is still occupied with some material object or other. He is still the indefatigable young explorer, still investigating the world around him, still studying the objects he finds in it. One day you will find him absorbed in the stones of the gravel path, picking them up, perhaps, and putting them in a tin can. ("Pong!" what a satisfactory noise each stone makes as he drops it in!) Another day he has found a caterpillar on the garden path—what an excitement! How thrilling to watch it move forward in living waves of locomotion. Again, what a delight simply to pour water from one vessel to another and back again, *ad infinitem!* His life, in fact, is a continuous series of the most absorbing scientific experiments. But, alas, how often you may see these young scientists dragged away from their researches by some inexorable adult, as they still cling to their latest discovery — a shell, perhaps, or a bit of colored paper. (A young friend of mine, aged two, was invited once to have a ride on a merry-go-round at a country fair. He accepted, on condition that I would hold his latest treasure, which he carried shut up in his chubby hand. Ignorant of what was there, I promised to do so. Whereupon, opening his small, hot fingers, he presented me with an energetic beetle more than an inch long!)

We have long forgotten what it was like to be a child, when the world was all so new and wonderful and we ourselves endowed with such superabundant energy. Supposing a grown-up person, who had come to take tea with us, began to clamber onto the sideboard via the back of the sofa, or to wander around the room running his fingers along the contours of the tables and chairs, or began feeling, gently and seriously, curtains, cushion covers and even the texture of the clothes of those present; or suppose he amused himself opening and shutting the lid of the coal scuttle ten or twenty times running — we should feel considerably surprised. Yet to behave in this way would be quite natural and normal — one might almost say inevitable — in a child of three.

No sensible person, least of all Montessori, would deny that there are plenty of occasions when children should be restrained. But the tragedy of it is that grownups, as a whole, do not yet realize either the importance or the significance of this profound instinct which urges children to such constant and active exploration. They regard it simply as a bothersome tendency to "meddle with everything," "to fiddle about with things." The child is, in fact, "a disturber of the peace"—the peace of adults, of course — and should learn "to be good and keep still" — as if goodness and immobility were synonymous.

On the other hand, Dr. Montessori, who always observes nature and follows her, instead of trying to suppress these instincts, recognizes them as God-given and endeavors to allow them the fullest play, harnessing them to educational purposes. Thus, to take but one example, the child who takes such a delight in touching things and feeling their shapes is given a whole alphabet of sandpaper letters (each letter mounted on a separate card) and he is encouraged to feel around them *ad lib* with his first and second fingers — i.e., the writing fingers. After a few weeks or months, this exercise, when combined with certain other occupations equally suited to his age and interests, leads to a most dramatic result — the explosion into writing. Those who are interested should read the graphic description given by Montessori herself in *The Secret of Childhood*, pages 148-150.

We adults should learn, then, to accustom ourselves to think of the child not as *il disturbatore* but as *l'exploratore* (not as the disturber but as the explorer) whose motto is:

"The world is so full of a number of things
I'm sure we should all be as happy as kings."

THE SENSORIAL FOUNDATION OF THE LIFE OF THE INTELLECT

It is not only "things" that interest children, but also the *qualities* of things — such as roughness, redness, emptiness, littleness and so forth. At the Mad Hatter's tea party, the Dormouse asks Alice: "Did you ever see a muchness?" The answer was, quite rightly, in the negative, for muchness is an abstract quality and, as such, can never be seen or felt or touched or known by any sense, but "seen" only by the mind. With our eyes we can only see "much," i.e., a definite quantity, of a particular commodity — sugar, sand, etc.

At this point we touch (with the mind, of course) upon one of the most important principles underlying the whole Montessori system, one which illuminates and explains this trait in children, i.e., their passionate interest in concrete and material objects.

How did we grownups obtain our ideas of roughness, smoothness, squareness, muchness, and the like? We do

not remember when or how. As the poet says:
> "Who knows the individual hour in which
> His habits first were sown, even as a seed?
> Who shall point as with a wand and say
>   'This portion of the river of my mind
>   Came from yon fountain.'?"

Nevertheless one thing is certain. We got our idea of smoothness from smooth objects, of squareness from square objects, of sharpness from sharp objects (probably accompanied by painful experiences). Since the time of Aristotle, it has been recognized that "there is nothing in the intellect that was not first in the senses."

Theoretically it is possible to conceive of intellectual beings who do not gain their ideas through the senses. Such precisely, according to theologians, is the nature of the angel's mind. Being pure spirits (i.e., without material bodies), they *could not* have sensations, for these are experiences possible only to a mind linked to a material body. Therefore, if angels have ideas, and, from what has been revealed of their duties, it is certain that they have them, these ideas must have been infused into them in some other way.

Be that as it may, with us human beings the case is different. The newborn baby (in spite of what Kant says) has no ideas, any more than a newborn cat. But man alone among the animals (Aristotle defined man as "a rational animal") has the power to create them. And upon this power is based his "sovereignty of reason" — that "capable and godlike faculty." For it would be impossible to reason without the power to make and compare judgments and judgments would be impossible without abstract ideas.

There is no more fascinating psychological study than the manner in which the intellect, availing itself of the materials supplied by the senses, creates these abstract ideas, entities so immaterial that a mental image is gross by comparison with them; yet entities so formidable that Plato regarded them (wrongly) as the ultimate realities, the prototypes, from which all material "copies" are derived.

But we must not let the philosophical aspects of the question detain us here. As teachers, we are concerned with the *fact* of this sensorial foundation of the life of the intellect, and with the practical considerations which arise from it.

In the history of education from Comenius, through Rousseau, Pestallozzi and Froebel, down to the present day, there has been an increasing tendency to help the child in building his ideas by means of sensible objects. But no one has so completely incorporated this principle into a system of education as has Dr. Montessori.

SPONTANEOUS ASCENT FROM CONCRETE TO ABSTRACT

It is indeed a common criticism of the Montessori method that it goes too far in this direction; that it places an overemphasis on the concrete. There is a danger (such critics say) that, surrounded as he is in the Montessori school by so many tangible and material objects, the intellectual progress of the child may be retarded. Like a tethered balloon his intellect must be, as it were, fastened down to all this didactic material, and prevented from soaring up into, and working freely in, its own realm of abstraction.

Dr. Montessori's experience, and that of her followers, shows that this fear is completely unfounded. The child's intellect is not like a balloon tethered to the ground. It can be much more aptly compared to an airplane which needs to run along the ground for some distance in order

51

to rise. When the right moment comes, the plane takes off from the solid ground, and soars into the more abstract medium of the air. Similarly the mind of the child, in order to rise into the abstract, has need of a preliminary contact with the material and concrete. But, when the right moment comes, it, too, takes off of its own accord, and rises into the realm of the abstract.

I once asked a child in a Montessori school I was visiting why she was not using the number frame (a kind of abacus) which lay idly on her table, to help in the long multiplication sums on which she was engaged. She answered simply and wisely: "Because I can do them quicker without it." Her mind had just "taken off" from the concrete material and needed it no longer.

This spontaneous ascent from the concrete to the abstract occurs when two factors are present: *First,* a certain general maturity of mind, and *second,* a great clarity with regard to the particular concrete process in question. In the case just mentioned, it was multiplication by several figures.

A much more real and common danger in education lies, not in holding the mind too long in contemplation of the concrete, but in hurrying it forward, to attempt abstract reasonings and calculations before it has had sufficient acquaintance with the concrete—i.e., before it has attained that inner maturity and clarity of mind of which we have just spoken.

How many persons, to the end of their lives, harbor vague and incomplete notions about arithmetical operations (their shopping change, for instance) simply because, in their early lessons in arithmetic, they were rushed into doing more and ever more abstract calculations before they had clearly mastered (by the help of concrete examples) those fundamental relations upon which all subsequent work depends? Nowhere has Montessori's insight shown itself more clearly than in devising the beautiful and carefully graded materials for teaching number, and the four rules, and many operations such as square and cubic root, and the beginnings of algebra and geometry. It is a remarkable fact, but undeniably true, that it has never been known that any child in a Montessori school has disliked arithmetic — provided he came there at three and a half years and worked through all the materials from the beginning.

ANOTHER REASON WHY LIBERTY IS SO ESSENTIAL

In connection with this spontaneous ascent of the intellect from the concrete to the abstract, it is worth while to point out another reason why it is so important that liberty should be given the child — liberty, in the sense that Dr. Montessori uses the word. In the Montessori school there is no hard and fast rule that such and such sums must be done with the aid of this or that material, or by such and such time, or that so many sums must be done with the material first, and then so many without. The child is left free to decide these matters for himself and he can do it better than anyone else. As soon as he feels that the didactic material has become a hindrance rather than a help, he simply leaves it behind, without asking anyone — just as, at a given moment, a baby learns to stand without holding on to an external support, and again without asking permission.

It is interesting to note that children often feel, inwardly, that it is quite an event when they discover that they *can* do their sums without the help of the material. Sometimes they will come up to the teacher and say with evident pride: "I did my sums today without using the frame!"

"Every mind," says Emerson, "is a system," and it is different from every other such system. Hence it is most unlikely that this inner ripening will take place at the same moment in a whole class, or, for that matter, even with two children. Thus we realize the value of individual work and of that liberty which permits the child to carry out to the full his cycle of work without interruption.

Children of the Gatehouse School in London singing to Dr. Montessori on her last visit to England, at the age of eighty. The Principal, Mrs. Wallbank, a leading Montessori expert in Britain, was a close friend of the "Dottoressa."

CHAPTER TWO
THE MONTESSORI INFANTS CLASS

THE AGE OF SENSORY-MOTOR ACTIVITY

THE MONTESSORI INFANTS CLASS CORRESPONDS to a period in the child's development when interest in the sensory qualities of things still predominates. Hence the visitor to this class will find many of the children occupied with the elementary sensorial materials — e.g., the Pink Tower, the cylinders, Broad Stair, Long Stair, sound boxes, color tablets, geometric insets, and so on. These are the materials which make the strongest appeal to the children of three and a half to four years when thy first come to school — these and the materials for doing the exercises in practical life.

THE ISOLATION OF STIMULUS

What makes the sensorial materials at once so effective and so fascinating is the brilliant manner in which Montessori has been able to isolate the particular sensory stimulus in question — whether it be length, magnitude, color or pitch. This she has done by making the various objects in each series *identical in every aspect except that particular quality on which the mind is being concentrated.*

We should notice, too, that every one of these sensorial materials not only stimulates sensory impressions, but also sets going a motor activity. There is always something to *do* as well as to see, hear, feel, etc. This is very important, for it is just this movement that helps to rivet the child's attention and enables him to concentrate for a long period on that particular form of order which is implicit in each material. Hence we call this epoch in the child's life not simply an age of sensory interests but sensory-*motor* activities.

THE EXERCISES OF PRACTICAL LIFE

In the Montessori infants class great use is made of the exercises of practical life. In addition to seeing the children work with sensorial materials, the visitor is sure to see a number of them busily engaged in such occupations as dusting the materials and furniture, sweeping the floor, watering the plants, arranging flowers, scrubbing the tables with soap and water, etc. If it is before lunch time, she may see a group of infants peeling potatoes, spreading butter on bread, or setting the table. If lunch is in progress she will probably see some of the children acting as waiters to the rest. After lunch it will very likely be the children who clear away the things, wash them, dry them and put them away. Besides activities of this sort which have to do with keeping their environment in order, there are also many others which are directed to the care of the children's own persons. Some will be seen washing their hands — a long ritual — others brushing their hair (or another child's hair, as often happens with the older ones), others again may be doing a bit of manicure, or, perhaps, cleaning and polishing a pair of shoes, or brushing a coat.

Now these exercises of practical life (and with them we include the exercises of balance and the silence game) are in Montessori s opinion just as important, from the point of view of mental development and equilibrium of character, as the sensorial materials or the lessons in reading, writing and arithmetic. Their paramount importance lies in the fact that the small child, to use Montessori's striking phrase, it still "incompletely incarnated." He is a creature composed of soul and body, but the soul is still incompletely incarnated. The soul, as the spiritual element, is potentially the dominant partner. But the fact remains that, at this stage, the mind is linked with a body which should be the instrument for carrying out its purposes, but is still incapable of doing so. As Montessori puts it, the trouble with the small child is that "the spirit is willing but the flesh is weak." By the "flesh" in this context, Montessori does not mean it in the Scriptural sense — i.e., a body imperfect through the effects of original sin. It simply means a complicated muscular system which is as yet imperfectly co-ordinated.

This "flesh" is "weak" only because it lacks the very complicated co-ordination of a great number of muscles which is essential to the carrying out of delicate movements. Therefore, one of the small child's most urgent needs is to have the opportunity — repeated and continuous opportunities — for carrying out complicated actions directed toward intelligent ends. This explains the secret of the intense and serious joy which the children display as they perform these exercises of practical life. That it is not the achievement of the external end which gives them such satisfaction is seen from the fact that a child will often wash the same table all over again the moment he has finished. The real aim of these exercises is *internal* — to develop a more complete unity between body and mind, to enrich the personality with more power and efficiency, and thus to present it with an ever more perfect instrument for carrying out its wishes.

ORDERED MOVEMENTS

We have said this is an age of sensory-motor activities, and now we see why these motor activities are so essential — i.e., because the child is incompletely incarnated. That is why every occupation in the Montessori classroom involves some sort of bodily movement. But by movement we do not mean random movement. It must be ordered movement, directed to some intelligent end. Each of these exercises of practical life has a definite purpose. Furthermore, the various actions leading to these ends are made even more clear by what Montessori calls "the logical analysis of movement." This sounds very learned and complicated, but it is really quite simple. It merely means that the teacher, in presenting the action to be done, divides it into its component parts and at the same time points out — by doing it — how one part logically comes before another. Thus, in opening the door, it is important to complete the movement of turning the handle before pulling the door toward you. Awkward and disordered movements generally result from attempting one part of a complicated movement before the previous one has been completed.

MOVEMENT COMBINED WITH INTELLIGENCE

We have already noted how the proper use of each of the sensorial materials involves a muscular activity such as sorting, comparing and arranging. But this is equally true of all the later materials — those for learning arithmetic or spelling or grammar. These intellectual occupations are almost always accompanied by movement — at least in the beginning. It is always a case of learning by doing something in the concrete — even if you are learning the formula $(a+b)^2 = a^2 + 2ab + b^2$; or taking the square root of a number like 1296. Aristotle taught that there is nothing in the intellect which was not first in the senses. If he had been an observer in a Montessori class, he would have added "there is nothing in the intellect which was not in the senses *plus movement*." Or at any rate he would have made it clear that his dictum included the muscular sense as well as the usual "five gateways to the soul."

DAWNING OF THE NEXT STAGE

Though the majority of the children in the Montessori infants class are occupied either with the exercises of practical life or with the sensorial materials, you will generally find some of the older ones already busy with those materials which are directly concerned with teaching the first steps in the three "R's." Thus you may find some of them busy touching the letters and at the same time saying out loud the sounds they represent. Others may be learning numbers, or even doing little sums with the number rods; others, again, doing "odds and evens" with little discs. Some may be putting out the "spindles" (another number exercise). Very probably you will see two or three of them composing phonetic words on a mat with movable letters, while others are making designs with the metal insets and coloring them with crayons — an occupation which forms an indirect preparation for writing.

TRANSITION FROM INFANTS TO ELEMENTARY SCHOOL

There is no definite outward break to mark the child's transition from the infants class to the elementary school stage. He does not pass from one room to another; still less does he form part of a group that is collectively transferred to another teacher. Montessori did not believe in that sort of equal grading, even if it were possible. She liked to have children of different ages working together. Not, of course, the *very* youngest with the *very* oldest, but she finds it is best to have an overlapping of two or three different age groups. Thus children of ages four to six could very well work together, or children from five to seven years. The reason for this overlapping is that — when children are left to work freely on their own — they are constantly helping one another. Those who are less advanced appeal to those who know more, and these latter are always willing to give their assistance. In this way, knowledge in a Montessori school takes wings and flies from one child to another independently of the teacher. This is an excellent thing, not only from the point of view of the advancement of learning, but also socially and morally. Under ordinary school conditions, children often have little opportunity of showing mutual aid instead of competition; and sometimes, when they do try to help each other, they are hindered from doing so by the teacher — at times even punished for it.

But to return to the question of a child's transition from the infants class stage to that of the elementary school. As this change takes place in a Montessori school, it can best be described as an inner episode in the life of a developing individual, But though there is no outward and definite break in the child's life to mark this transition, the directress will nevertheless be well aware of it. She will have noticed that the child tends more and more, now, to choose such materials as the movable letters for composing words; or the number rods, or sandpaper letters, or the golden decimal system beads. She will have observed, too, that he works with these for longer periods, while, at the same time, he becomes correspondingly less interested in the purely sensorial occupations. This indicates that the child is passing, or has already passed, into the next stage of his mental development in which he is concerned more directly with the elements of culture, i.e., reading, writing, arithmetic, geometry, geography, etc..

What happens now? Does the teacher group the children into classes, provide them with reading and arithmetic primers and copybooks, and teach them collectively as in ordinary schools? *Deo gratias,* no. Things go on just as before. The children continue to work by themselves, individually, except every now and then, when they form spontaneously into little groups to work together.

But, in practice, how is this accomplished? How can children spontaneously teach themselves those types of knowledge which, in the ordinary way, are only acquired (and that with much trouble) by the combined efforts of the children and the teacher? Indeed, how could it be possible for a child to teach himself what he does not yet know? The solution of this apparent anomaly is to be found in the presence, in a Montessori class, of what we might call the *new third factor in education.* In the ordinary classroom there are two main elements or factors — the children and the teacher. The teacher teaches and the children learn from her — and that is that! But, under the Montessori system, there enters upon the scene this new third factor of equal importance to the teacher. This is the *prepared environment.*

THE NEW THIRD FACTOR IN EDUCATION — THE PREPARED ENVIRONMENT

No one who has not seen a properly equipped Montessori classroom can form any adequate conception of the amount of loving care, intellectual labor and inventive

61

genius which has been put into the construction of this specially prepared environment. Everything in that environment has been so constructed as to correspond with the stature — physical, mental, social and spiritual — of children, not of adults. Indeed, in many cases, the very house itself has been specially constructed to suit the proportions of children, not of adults. Such "children's houses" are built with low windows, small doors and stairs with steps of a very small gradient. Cloakrooms, lavatories, cupboards, etc., all are on a Lilliputian scale. Such a house is truly a *casa dei bambini* (a children's house). In the rooms and corridors all the furniture and appurtenances are constructed on the same diminutive scale. There are small low tables with tiny chairs to match. Cupboards are so low they come only up to your knees. All around the classroom you will see many of these long, low cupboards, the shelves of which are laden with a wide variety of specially constructed didactic materials. Each of these has its own place on the shelves and its own purpose. All the materials are (under certain conditions) at the disposal of all the children. In fact, nothing is allowed to enter this prepared environment which is not going to be of use, at some stage, in the child's mental and social development.

It would take a book — several books, in fact — to describe all the teaching materials to be found in a Montessori classroom, materials which vary according to the age of the children. We shall not attempt even a brief account of them here. But it is important to notice that the presence of all these materials makes individual work possible. Without these the children would not be able to work away as they do for hours, quite happily and quite independently of the teacher. I have sometimes, when observing in Montessori schools, seen children of seven years of age who have literally worked the whole morning without once consulting the teacher.

This means that, in a Montessori school, the teacher does not teach the children directly and collectively; but indirectly and individually through the teaching materials, or, to put it another way, through what we have called the new third factor — the prepared environment.

We must, however, guard against a misunderstanding at this point. When we say that the children are learning from the materials, and not from the teacher, we do not mean to say that the teacher *never* teaches the children directly. She is bound to do this, at intervals, with each child (or groups of children) in order to explain how to use the materials. The directress is, in fact, the dynamic link between the children and the prepared environment with all its varied teaching occupations. But, once the directress sees that any child has learned to use a new piece of material, her job for the time being is completed. Like a hostess who has introduced two guests to each other, she retires into the background, glad to see them enjoying each other's company, and thankful to have been the means of bringing about such a friendship.

In the case of the child and the new piece of material this "friendship" may continue for many weeks. It will continue in fact until the child has outgrown that particular material and has learned all that it has to teach him at this stage. He is now ready for something more advanced.

WHAT MAKES THE MONTESSORI CLASS GO?

To one who has never visited a Montessori school before, the first impression is of something almost miraculous. We are so accustomed to think of children as creatures who prefer play to work; who in fact can only be made to work by enticement, cajolery or coercion, that—when we see a whole roomful of children all seriously, continuously and spontaneously working away without any incentive from without — it quite amazes us. We are obliged to reverse our ideas of the capacities and characteristics of childhood. As we watch this astonishing scene, we ask ourselves what makes it go? What is the *élan*, the driving force, behind this immense and manifold labor of both body and mind?

It is not a simple thing, but a compound of several elements, each of which must be used in its right proportion. Otherwise the system doesn't work properly.

STREAMS OF MENTAL ENERGY

By far the most fundamental and important of these elements is the spontaneous intellectual energy of the child. Without this mysterious and constant stream of natural energy, the system would not work at all. It would be better, perhaps, if we used the plural and said "these mysterious streams of mental energy." For each child is such a stream.

The important thing to bear in mind in trying to understand the *élan* of a Montessori class is the realization that this precious stream of mental energy, which exists in each child, is strictly limited. There is only just so much of it and no more — though the actual amount varies with each child and with the same child at different times.

Just because it is so very limited, we must take the greatest care not to waste it. We must not expect it to work miracles — "it can't do more than it can." The wonderful point about Dr. Montessori's method is that she has mastered the secret by which we can make the best and fullest use of this spontaneous mental energy, so that none of it is dissipated, but all of it is directed into constructive channels.

Perhaps we can make this point clearer by way of contrast. Let us imagine ourselves to be in an ordinary kindergarten or elementary class when the teacher goes out of the room. Do the children continue working with the same concentration and discipline as when the teacher was in it? By no means. If she is absent for any length of time, the disorder will often increase until bedlam reigns. On the other hand, as I have seen many times and in different lands, if the directress leaves a Montessori classroom the children continue to carry on with their work just the same. Why is this? Is it because the Montessori children are endowed with more intelligence than the others? Not at all. Those children who are fooling about and creating bedlam because the teacher is away have just as much intelligence. In each of them, too, runs this wonderful stream of intellectual energy, for it is a normal human endowment. Wherein then lies the cause of the enormous and striking difference? It is found in the circumstance that — owing to the presence of the third factor, the prepared environment in the Montessori classroom and the children's relation to it — none of this mental energy is being dissipated in disorderly and useless activity. Every scrap of it is being canalized into the construction of personality. This intellectual energy is, in fact, being used for the purpose for which it was created — viz., to enable the individual possessing it to build up an orderly system of knowledge. Instead of being squandered in a host of disorderly and useless activities, such as pulling Janet's hair, or throwing spit balls at Tommy, or mere chatter — as in the case of the disorderly class — the mental energy of each child in the Montessori school is canalized along one or other of the many interesting and instructive occupations which form a part of the prepared environment. In short, the outward cause of the difference lies in the presence in the Montessori schoolroom (and not in the other classroom) of the third factor. The directress has gone out, it is true, but the third factor remains; whereas in the ordinary school, when the teacher goes out, only one factor remains — the children. To abandon children to their own devices is not the same thing as educating them through liberty, because you *cannot* give them true liberty without placing them in a prepared environment.

HOW THE INTELLECT WORKS — A PRINCIPLE OF ORDER

The intellect is the principle of order in mental development. It is of its very essence to create order, and it does so by seeking and binding together like with like, and like with unlike, according to the principles of identity and contrast. The very name, intellect, indicates its mode of action, coming as it does from the Latin *legere* (to bind). Or the intellect can be compared to a light in whose presence we are enabled to discern distinctions where (before its advent) all was darkness and confusion.

Although it is true that, by the time he comes to three years of age, the child's intellect has achieved a prodigious construction (when compared with the "nothing" with which it started), yet it is also true that there still remains, outside and beyond that part of the world which it has explored and mapped out, a vast and unexplored region where ignorance and confusion still reign. As Montessori puts it: "The child of three still carries within him a heavy chaos." He is still the young explorer, and every day he finds himself constantly coming up against unexplained mysteries, unrelated experiences and puzzling anomalies.

All sorts of ideas and images jostle in his mind without

logical connection. (A young friend of mine—aged five—said to his mother: "I sneezed and the clock stopped!") The child's immature intelligence is still as active as ever, trying to extend the bounds of its cosmos at the expense of this inner and outer chaos, endeavoring constantly to bring ever more and more objects, facts and experiences under the reign of law and order.

It is a hard task, this, of trying to understand the world in which he lives (we none of us ever complete it!) yet the child's mind carries on undaunted in spite of the appalling perplexity of it all.

But, as stated above, the stream of mental energy in the child who has to tackle this work is very limited. And so our efforts as educators should be directed into helping him to do it as quickly, easily and efficiently as possible.

ORDER IMPLICIT IN THE PREPARED ENVIRONMENT

It is just at this point that we see the immense importance of the prepared environment as a help to the child's intellectual development. The intellect seeks order in its sensations with regard to color, shape, size, texture, etc.; order in its mental images; order in the words it has picked up; order in its ideas of quantity, time and so forth. Now in the prepared environment it finds what it is seeking, for the prepared environment is the veritable home of order. Everything in it has been put there just because it contains order and relationship, whether implicit or explicit. Nothing irrelevant is permitted to exist there—nothing *dis*-orderly.

Take the sensory materials, for instance, the color tablets, the cylinders, the sound boxes—any one you like—and you will find that through each of them there runs a principle of order. In fact, you *cannot* use them correctly without respecting the principle of order which is inherent in each of them.

PREPARED PATHS TO CULTURE

So the child's intellect discovers (and discovers with great joy) the various forms of ordered knowledge which lie waiting for it, hidden like precious veins of gold, stored within the various occupations in the prepared environment. In this connection, too, we should not forget the exercises of practical life—for their object also is to create order. This is true in a double sense: first, co-ordination in the child's sensory-muscular system, and, secondly, preservation of the outward order in the prepared environment.

It is one of the first duties of the Montessori directress to see that the order in the prepared environment is preserved down to the smallest detail. For, as Montessori says, the child learns to appreciate order and to become orderly —down to the roots of his being—not through the direct exhortations of the teacher, but indirectly through the influence of the order in the prepared environment.

ORDER IN THE ADVANCED MATERIALS

But this spontaneous search of the child's intellect for order—or rather the search of his whole being, mind and body, for orderly activity—does not cease when he has outgrown the sensorial materials. The intelligence must always continue to seek for order by its very nature. Was it not Aristotle who maintained that, unless there are obstacles in the way, a faculty must go on working? And the intellect, other things being equal, can no more cease to work than the eye can cease to see. No longer satisfied with the raw materials provided by the sensorial occupations, the child's intellect seeks new worlds to conquer— more objects to relate, more concepts to put in order. And in the wonderful prepared environment it finds them in abundance. This is only another way of saying that the Montessori school is the young explorer's paradise.

THE PREPARED PATHS LEAD TO MORE ORDER

In what forms does the child, who has left the sensorial material behind him, discover these "varied and never ending successions of order" in the prepared environment? He finds them in that form which we might describe as the prepared paths to culture. Each of these is a pathway of research leading toward some definite school subject. And all these paths radiate from the sensorial materials. Every such path contains within it a principal of order.

Take arithmetic for example. What is arithmetic, in essence, but a continuation—into ever more minute particulars—of the study of the relationship between quantities; a study, be it observed, already begun by the child on the sensorial plane, through his work with the cylinders, Broad and Long Stairs, etc.? What is learning to spell, especially in a phonetic language, but a study of the relationships which exist between certain sounds and certain symbols? Grammar, too, is a study of order; of the order to be found in words, either in their inflections or in their relationships one to another in a sentence. Similarly, geometry, what is it essentially but a study of the relationship between geometric figures, themselves *ordered* shapes which have already been studied sensorially in the geometric cabinet? So what happens then, in actual practice, is that—as soon as the child has passed beyond the purely sensorial stage—he finds himself traveling along one or other of these paths to culture. One leads to writing, another to reading, a third to arithmetic, a fourth to grammar, others to nature study, geography, history, music, and so forth.

Along each of these paths the child finds waiting for him a carefully graded series of interesting and ingenious occupations, so devised that they illuminate, step by step, that form of order which is characteristic of the particular field of culture it represents.

The successive occupations along each path are so skillfully devised and so perfectly graded that—provided the child has been taught how to use them properly and is prevented from misusing them—he is able to make progress, at his own pace and by himself, with a minimum of assistance from the directress.

LEARNING BY DISCOVERY

We might point out that, for the child, a great deal of the fun of this procedure arises from the fact that he may, suddenly and unexpectedly, arrive at some—to him—quite unknown port, all on his own. He is, in fact, still in an exact sense of the word an explorer. For, thanks to the genius of Montessori, matters are so arranged that he can still acquire a great deal of knowledge *spontaneously and by discovery.*

This is not a mere metaphor. It is a literal fact, as any experienced Montessori directress would tell you. Again and again it happens that, as the children work away quietly with the materials, they make sudden discoveries for themselves. When this occurs, it brings an indescribable thrill of joy to the child concerned. These sudden inspirations are what we term Montessori explosions.

ANALYSIS AND ISOLATION OF DIFFICULTIES

The first thing to be done in teaching any subject through autoeducation is to analyze the various difficulties and then present each difficulty in isolation. But not only this; we must present each of the difficulties, so isolated, by means of an occupation which forms a complete and interesting whole in itself.

We have already emphasized the point that the precious stream of mental energy in each child is very limited, and so we must never expect him to do too much at once. Hence this principle of isolating the difficulties. Each separate difficulty must be, as it were, incarnated in a material specially designed to illuminate it, a material, be it remembered, which is not just something to be looked at and then put on one side, but something which elicits in the child a long continued activity of hand as well as brain.

THIS ANALYSIS IS PSYCHOLOGICAL, NOT LOGICAL

Another vital principle is this: in analyzing and separating the difficulties involved in any subject, our aim is to seek and find them according to their psychological order, rather than along the lines of their inherent logic. This means that the order of presentation of any part of the subject depends not so much on a logical approach to that subject as on a study of the sensitive periods which happen to be dominant in the child's mind at any particular moment. Thus a Montessori child begins to study geometry at the age of four and a half, which most persons would think far too early. At this stage, however, the study of geometry is done at a sensorial level and not by means of abstract reasoning—as anyone can see who watches these tiny children busy with the wooden geometric insets. It would be useless, at this stage, to begin with definitions and axioms, or even abstract descriptions of geometric figures. On the other hand, it is quite clear that the sensorial study of geometric forms, by means of the wooden insets, answers a felt need of children at this age. At the same time it creates a valuable preparation for a deeper knowledge of the same figures at a later date, and on a higher level.

To illustrate this point still further, let us consider how the Montessori child learns to write. He begins to tackle this subject by means of the sandpaper letters at the age of four to four and a half. Not later, because that is the sensitive period in which the child takes great delight in studying forms and shapes by means of the sense of touch. Similarly, following the psychological, not the logical, order, we find that free children spontaneously learn to write before they learn to read. In fact a child of four and a half to five will often be unable to read the word which he himself has spontaneously composed with the movable alphabet a quarter of an hour before.

To take one more example at random. A child of five years will learn how to count, with the golden bead material, in tens, hundreds and thousands, before he can write the numbers ten to twenty. Thus we see that, in each subject, the child learns certain things pertaining to it on different levels of thought, according to the nature of the sensitive period which is dominant at the moment. That is what we mean by saying that the order of the presentation of the elements of any subject depends upon a psychological rather than a logical analysis.

If we thus follow the psychological, rather than the logical, order we shall obviate certain difficulties which often arise in ordinary schools, especially with children who begin school late. In the Montessori class, where children begin their progress along these paths to culture at an unusually early age, the more mechanical aspects of the subject are well mastered before the higher and more intellectual aspects come on the scene. To explain by an illustration: it not infrequently happens, in an ordinary school, that a boy—especially if he begins school rather late

—may arrive at the age of ten or eleven without having acquired a good handwriting or a knowledge of the elements of spelling. Such a boy is in a sad plight, especially in a school where there is collective teaching, because he has arrived at a stage of mental maturity when he is naturally interested in more advanced matters, such as writing compositions, or grammar, or history. His self-expression in these subjects is hampered at every turn by his inadequate writing, spelling and reading—subjects in which he now has no interest, and which, because of his inefficency, give him a sense of inferiority (which only increases his distaste for them). Whereas, if he had learned to write sensorially at the age of four and a half or five, and learned spelling from long practice in composing words with the movable script letters and from phonogram cards, etc., at six to eight years, he would already have acquired such an efficiency in these matters as would liberate his mental energies at a later stage for more advanced forms of work—work congenial to his more advanced mental development. But, as it is, lacking this preparation in earlier and more mechanical foundations, he may be compared to a person with genuine musical ability who is unable to express himself on any instrument because he has never mastered the basic techniques.

PARALLEL EXERCISES

It must not be imagined that, because we have spoken of the occupations of each of the prepared paths as *carefully graded,* they are therefore arranged as it were in a single longitudinal series, each one just above the preceding one and below that which follows—in the manner that rules and exercises followed one another, step by step, in the old-fashioned arithmetic primers. It would be more accurate to say that on these prepared paths there is a *group* of similar exercises at each stage, all on the same level, and all dealing more or less with the same difficulty in different ways.

This is what Montessori calls the principle of parallel exercises. An example will make this clearer. Suppose a child is at the stage of learning the four different operations in arithmetic, and suppose he is doing the sum: 2,346

$$+ 1,475$$

He can do this in at least six different ways: (1) With the golden beads of the decimal system, (2) with the number frame, (3) with the short bead stair on a piece of cloth with four columns, (4) with the stamp numbers, (5) by the dot game,* and, finally, without the help of anything concrete and visible. A casual visitor, watching him at work, doing the same sum in all these various ways, might very easily think he was doing as many entirely different operations, because they *appear* so different externally. But actually it is the very same operation he is doing, through differing media, that is, by different concrete aids.

Why bother to complicate the matter in this way? you might ask. We do so because it is a great help to see the same operation done under such widely differing forms. Doing it through these various media makes the common element, which is the very essence of the operation, the vital part, stand out much more vividly and clearly than if it were seen under only one guise. It is not, of course, necessary that every child should work through all these parallel exercises. Some minds are naturally quicker and more penetrating than others, and these comprehend principles more quickly and from fewer examples. But there is no doubt whatever that, generally speaking, this princi-

*For a more complete explanation of these didactic materials see Part Two

ple of parallel exercises greatly helps the child's mind to grasp the essential nature of the operation they are designed to illustrate.

SPONTANEOUS MENTAL EXPANSION

The effect of the child's spontaneous working with these parallel exercises is very interesting and somewhat surprising. It happens, again and again, that the child, who has been working for a long time at a group of parallel exercises all on the same plane, suddenly and with a flash of intuition becomes aware of some truth, law or principle which he had not known before. It is a genuine, spontaneous, inspiration and it has been brought about in the following way: To judge purely by what one sees externally, it would seem that, all the time the child has been working through these parallel exercises, his mind has remained at the same level. But actually, during all that period, psychic energy has been storing up. It is this that causes the sudden illumination, which, when it comes, lifts the mind to a higher level. One might compare the way this happens to the gradual raising of a barge, while it remains stationary in a canal lock, until the moment comes when it finds itself on a higher level. The lock gates are then opened, and it now proceeds further, but on that new and higher level. Such flashes of illumination—which we usually associate with the inspirations of genius—form, according to Montessori, the manner in which the child's mind should normally expand; and it does so expand, given the right conditions. This was her considered judgment after thirty years of experience with "normalized" children, and every experienced Montessori directress would agree with her.

A young boy, aged six, in my class, once went around informing every member of it that "Three eights make twenty-four. *Nobody told me.* Three eights make twenty-four. *Nobody told me.*" The "nobody told me" seemed to him even more wonderful than the truth revealed.

THE PRINCIPLE OF THE HOOK
I remember once how Dr. Montessori, in the middle of one of her lectures, drew a hook on the board, like this:

and then made the remark that it symbolized one of the important principles of her method. In this manner she wished to draw attention to the fact that there exists in her system a sort of invisible or mental "hook" which links each piece of the teaching material to something which is to follow at a later stage. Or, to express it in another way, though each of the materials is an end in itself, it also contains something which foreshadows and prepares the way for what will follow later. For example, Montessori insists that the child of three and a half *must* be made to manipulate the cylinders by holding them by the little knob at the top, between the thumb and first two fingers of the right hand. The directress must insist on this, even if the child naturally tends to grasp the cylinders with the whole hand. Why this interference with the child's liberty? "Because is is the hand of a civilized being who is soon going to learn to write, and this forms an indirect preparation for holding a pencil."

In the same way, the many hours which the smaller children spend filling in, with colored crayons, the designs they have made with the metal insets, form an indirect preparation for writing, since they constitute an excellent practice in holding and manipulating a pencil. This is also one of the reasons the directress should insist that the filling-in lines be parallel, since this requires more control, making it an even better preparation for writing. It is just these preparatory exercises, done without any conscious connection with the idea of writing, which — along with others such as feeling the sandpaper letters—pave the way for the "explosion" into writing that often occurs at a later stage .

Let us take one more example. The child of three and a half to four years who works away with the various sensory materials, known as the Pink Tower, Broad Stair and Long Stair, is building better than he knows. Although he himself is concerned only with how to build the Pink Tower, or how to arrange the steps of the Long Stair in their proper order, he is also at the same time unconsciously making his first acquaintance with certain truths which will come to mean much more to him at a later stage. Thus, the smallest cube in the Pink Tower has a volume equal to one cubic centimeter, the largest equals a liter, while the longest rod is one meter in length—all units of measurement in science. The small child does not know these facts; nor do we tell them to him. But, later on, when he comes to learn about the continental decimal system of measurement, he will find himself on ground already familiar and will recognize with joy the old friends he used to play with "years ago" in the infants class.

This organic relationship between the earliest materials and a more advanced knowledge at a later stage is another example of that mental order which is implicit in the prepared environment. It is also one of the features which distinguishes the Montessori materials form the Froebelian gifts .

THE MINIMUM DOSE

The aim of the teacher in an ordinary school is to teach the child as much as he can, but the aim of the Montessori directress, on the other hand, is to teach the children as little as she can. Her aim is, in fact, to give the child what Montessori calls "the minimum dose" of teaching.

This apparent absurdity is easily understood if one bears in mind that in the Montessori system there exists the third factor, the prepared environment, which is as important in its own way as the teacher herself. It does not follow that, because the Montessori directress aims at giving the child a minimum of *direct* instruction, she therefore wishes the child to remain in ignorance. Her attitude is based on the maxim that it is always better if the child can teach himself—that is, learn by his own active experience. In this way he genuinely apprehends or grasps knowledge by an active assimilation, instead of a passive receiving. This active apprehension is just what the child's long-continued and spontaneous concentration on the materials enables him to achieve. Without it the child would necessarily be dependent on the teacher for his knowledge. (You might say "Why not a book?". Because, in actual experience, it must be remembered that the child cannot teach himself by means of the materials unless he already has been instructed in their proper use. To this extent, therefore, it is essential that the directress should instruct the child directly. She is the link between the children and the prepared environment.)

And, further, she must be a dynamic link. For if she performs her office in a dull and mechanical way, there will be no living "umbilical cord" between this "spiritual embryo" and the prepared environment whence he derives his mental nourishment. It is essential to emphasize this fact, for it is a point often misunderstood, or forgotten, that the materials, indeed the whole prepared environment, would be useless without the vivifying influence of the directress. An important part of her training consists in learning how to present the various materials in this living and dynamic manner.

The directress, in presenting the materials, must, however, carefully guard against giving too much. She must give just that amount of instruction that will stimulate the child's interest and activity, but no more. One of the golden maxims of the Montessori system, one which all parents as well as teachers should take to heart, is this: *Every useless aid arrests development.* Or, to put it another way: We adults should always act toward the child in such a way as to answer his unspoken prayer, *"Help me to do it myself."*

THE CONTROL OF ERROR

There is no more common misconception with regard to the Montessori system than the notion that, under it, children are "allowed to do anything they like." It is true enough that her system *is* based upon liberty. But to give the child liberty is not the same thing as abandoning him to his own devices and whims. This we shall see more clearly when we come to discuss the nature of that liberty granted to children in a Montessori school. Meanwhile we can say that anyone who realizes what a great importance Montessori attaches to the principle of the control of error would never fall into any such misconception regarding the child's liberty. The control of error is a principle which prevails through every department of the child's activities while at the Montessori school.

In an ordinary school the control of error resides chiefly, if not solely, in the teacher who, if she is conscientious, is careful about correcting the children's work and behavior. But in a classroom full of some forty children, all working individually at different occupations, how can the teacher be expected to correct every thing that every child does? That is why, whenever it is possible, especially in the earlier stages, Montessori has arranged things so that the control of error is to be found in the materials themselves, and in the general environment.

Take, for example, the various sets of cylinders. If a child makes a mistake in putting them back into their sockets, there is no need for the directress to point out the error. As the child comes to the end of the exercise the error reveals itself, for the last cylinder simply will not fit in anywhere. And so the mistake is realized and corrected without the directress even knowing about it.

Something similar happens in those exercises of practical life into which the teacher has inserted a motive of perfection. Thus a child, in setting the table, is recommended to put the cup down on the saucer without making a noise. If he does make a noise then, at once, he realizes he has made a mistake, and without anyone correcting him he repeats the movement more perfectly. The same thing happens when the child is told to pour water from one vessel to another without spilling a drop. The very furniture of a Montessori school is so constructed as to help the child by acting as a control of error. Thus Montessori insists that the little tables and chairs should be light and easily movable. Consequently, if a child in passing by another's table makes an awkward movement and jolts it, the table will move, causing annoyance to the child who is working at it. The idea behind this is not, of course, to promote the annoyance of others, but to bring home, automatically, to the clumsy child the awkwardness of his movements. As a consequence, next time he will keep a more careful watch over his movements and thus gradually, he perfects them by a more perfect co-ordination of muscles. In this way the very lightness and mobility of the tables act as a control of error, as also do vases of flowers placed on the tables. For a similar reason Montessori insists that the tables should be painted in some light color, so that, if the child has dirty fingers and smudges its surface, the dirt will show up. Then the child, realizing his untidiness, goes and gets a cloth and cleans away the dirt.

Of course, in some matters, the control of error lies principally with the directress, as, for instance, when a child is composing words with the movable alphabet on a mat on the floor. Yet even here the correction may come, in a very real sense, from the environment independently of the teacher. For it often happens that other children, who are more advanced, as they pass by notice a mistake in spelling; whereupon they pause for a moment, quite spontaneously, to point it out. The wrongly spelled word affects them just like dust or spilled water. It is something in their beloved environment that should not be there — and so they put it right.

Again, the materials themselves, by the very fact that they teach so clearly and make such a profound impression on the children's minds, constitute a form of control of error. They control it in the best possible way, by teaching the truth so accurately from the beginning that error has no chance to appear. This is particularly true of the arithmetical material. One day a new boy of eight was sent down to my class from a higher one, because he was "all in a muddle" with regard to subtraction. All that I needed to do was to introduce him to the units, tens, hundreds and thousands in the the bronze bead decimal system material with their corresponding number cards, and explain how to use them. After working out a number of examples with this material in the concrete, the whole of his erroneous complex of ideas vanished.

SECONDING NATURE

When we speak of the prepared paths to culture, each with its graded series of teaching materials, we must be careful not to fall into a misconception, as many do, of the real purpose of these materials. We must, in fact, distinguish between *teaching* by means of the materials and *assisting a natural development* by means of the materials. Right from the beginning of his life, the child's intelligence is spontaneously active. The small child, even the infant, is what Montessori calls an *essere assorbente,* a being who is continually absorbing impressions from the outside world. The *essere assorbente* becomes the young explorer as soon as he can walk. And, as he grows up, his mind — unless repressed and impeded — always continues to seek and absorb new knowledge from his environment. This is its very nature, and our business here, as always, is to second nature.

The child's mind, whether he ever goes to school or not, will develop and will build up a system of its own. What we aim at, through the materials, is to assist this natural tendency. We should regard the materials, then, not so much as difficulties to be overcome as helps to a development which is going on by its own energy, independently of us; one which will and must go on in any case. The materials help this spontaneous mental energy which, if left to itself in an *un*prepared environment, would find the struggle to create an orderly mental system beyond its strength. This is why Montessori often speaks of the prepared environment (which, of course, includes the directress) as a mental gymnasium in which the intellect, through exercising itself, grows ever stronger.

THE WHOLE AND THE PARTS

The intellect, as we have said, works by binding together the subject matter of thought in accordance with certain mental laws. It discovers "inner connections" (as Froebel used to call them) and, by means of these, builds up an orderly sytem, or, better still, groups of orderly systems. We can best assist this natural tendency if we present the various aspects of knowledge to the child, not in isolated fragments, but on the principle of presenting the whole and the parts together. Thus, in teaching any subject, or stage of a subject, we should give, first, an idea of the whole, in an ordered and comprehensive way, showing at the same time a general view of the interrelation of the parts, and, secondly, arrange things so that the child can now pass on to a study of the separate details. This, says Montessori, may seem to many persons to be an old-fashioned method, for the modern tendency is to eliminate classifications as too difficult. "It may *seem* old-fashioned," she goes on to say, "but all the same I think it will be the idea of the future."

In most subjects or aspects of knowledge, the child has already spontaneously grasped many details in isolation from the environment. But to see a system as a whole gives him a new understanding, which, for this very reason, brings a new interest. And this new interest acts as a stimulus to a further and more detailed study of the separate elements already seen in the environment.

Examine any of the Montessori sensory materials from this point of view and you will find that each is composed of a grouping of many sensations — visual, auditory or whatever the case may be — related together in an ordered whole. Thus the color tablets make a graded series from light to dark. The Long Stair makes a similar gradation in lengths from short to long, with all the intermediary steps thrown in. When done properly, the child builds a complete stair of ten steps.

This principle of presenting the whole and the parts does not cease with the sensory materials. It is carried on, all the way through, in one form or another. We come to a good example before the child has gone very far along the pathway of number.

As soon as the child has gained a clear idea of the numbers from one to ten and can recognize the symbols as well as the quantities, he is presented with Montessori's famous bird's-eye view of the decimal system with its units, tens, hundreds and thousands, from one to one thousand. It forms an impressive spectacle. It can, in fact, be compared to a view of the Promised Land into which he is about to enter and take possession. The child (aged four and a half to five and a half years) descends from this Pisgah of Vision filled with a great interest and enthusiasm to learn more about the separate details, and thereafter spends many days and weeks doing various exercises in counting and notation.

In the same way, a little later, a child who has made his "Table of Pythagoras" gets a new light on the multiplication tables, for, as he contemplates it *as a whole,* he is now led on to discover all sorts of interesting facts and comparisons, which he would never have realized had he only considered each multiplication table in isolation.

This seeing of a group of separate facts as a whole is not only interesting in itself, and therefore a stimulus to further research, but it is also an aid to memory. If you know the whole, even if you don't know, or have forgotten, some particular detail, you can find it out again for yourself just because you know its place in the whole.

It would be interesting to note here with what ingenuity Montessori applies this principle to the various subject matters of arithmetic, geometry, geography, history, grammar and so forth, but such a study would lead us far beyond the scope of this outline.

One more general point should, however, be mentioned: it may seem rather a truism, but it is really a further reflection on what we said earlier about the teacher being the dynamic link between the child and the prepared environment. Before the teacher can help the child by showing him these wholes with interrelated parts, the teacher herself must have thoroughly assimilated this principle in a vital and not merely mechanical way. Speaking on this subject once in a lecture on the early years of the secondary school, Montessori said, "the important thing is to give a cosmic idea, one complete whole, the universe, for the child's mind has now arrived at a more abstract stage, and seeks not only facts but their underlying causes, and you cannot properly see the connections until you have first seen the whole."

"But," she continued, "this is not so easy as simply to give the details. The difficulty resides not in the capacity of the child to understand but in the capacity of the teacher to present it.

"So we see it is not enough simply to love and understand the child; we must love and understand the universe. The teacher must first of all feel in herself a wonder and admiration for this universe in which we live, as a majestic whole. This is an essential part of the preparation of the teacher. Then she will know how to call to the soul of the awakened child. This is to be done, at this later stage, not as in the previous epoch through sensory-motor occupations, but by being able to render the knowledge to be acquired interesting and fascinating by presenting it as parts of one inspiring majestic whole."

INDEPENDENCE AND DEVELOPMENT

In several of her training courses, Montessori spoke at great length about the meaning of independence and its significance in development. With her, independence always has a biological significance. "Independence from a vital point of view means to be able to live without the immediate help of others." She was never tired of pointing out that true independence is a gradual achievement. In fact, the whole course of development can be described as the progressive acquisition by the individual of ever newer and higher forms of independence.

The acquisition of a new stage of independence means learning to do for yourself what, up to that time, someone else has done for you. From which it becomes clear that each new stage of independence in a developing organism corresponds to the acquisition of a new function.

In order to become a personality in the full sense of the word, the child must learn to feel, think, choose, decide, and, in general, act freely by himself. This is a law of nature, and we have already noted how children instinctively struggle to be allowed to do things for themselves. It is the imperious command of nature which urges them at almost any cost (and the cost is often very heavy) to act for themselves in a world which has *Verboten* plastered all over it. Thus, if we wish to second nature, we must stick closely to the maxim: *"Every useless aid, given to a growing organism, arrests development."*

A UNIVERSAL OPPRESSION

If we prevent children from carrying out those activities which are necessary for them — in order that they may acquire the forms of independence corresponding to their stages of development — we are heading straight for trouble, both for the children and for ourselves. It is in this manner that is engendered that struggle between the child and the adult of which Montessori speaks so frequently and so energetically. We can prevent the child from carrying out these activities — which are his right — either by doing too much for him ourselves, or by inhibiting his actions by the weight of our authority backed by persuasion or force.

Montessori maintains that the greater part of the naughtiness of children is not real naughtiness at all, i.e., in the sense of deliberate wickedness or even deliberate "cussedness." Their various forms of bad behavior represent, for the most part, the unconscious reactions of children to situations which they feel intuitively to be throttling their development. As Montessori very strongly puts it: "The child must either work or die." By "work" here she means any form of creative activity which helps to build up his personality.

The child develops his functions through activity and in no other way. Therefore, to deny him the possibilities of acting for himself is to cut at the very roots of his being. "Run upstairs," said the mother in *Punch*, "and see what Tommy is doing and *tell him not to*." That is only too often the adult attitude. The child, just because of his ceaseless activity, is looked upon as a disturber of the peace (the peace of the adult, of course). Yet so strong is the urge of nature within him to explore the world and find things out by his own sensory-motor activity that, in spite of prohibitions, he simply can't refrain from touching and handling the objects he finds about him. He *must* do this, for it constitutes for him the only way to fuller life and further development. Hence follow trouble, punishment and persecution.

According to Montessori, then, all over the world there is going on an oppression of the weak by the strong, of children by adults. Nor is it any less a real oppression because it is generally exercised unconsciously, or because those who persecute sincerely love those whom they are persecuting. Children, as a whole, form an oppressed class and one might describe the Montessori movement, from this point of view, as a struggle for the rights of children. It is a struggle to obtain for children the right to act for themselves, freely, according to the laws of development within them; the right to accomplish the great task of creating themselves, the men and women of the future.

The statement that there exists this universal oppression may strike many readers as fantastic exaggeration. But Montessori means it quite seriously and backs up her statement by the weight of thirty years' experience, both her own and that of her followers in a score of different countries. She has summed up this experience in her doctrine of normality and deviations.

DEVIATIONS FROM NORMALITY

The energies of growth, like all other energies, are indestructible. So when it happens that children are denied the true and proper use of these energies, these latter are not lost but become deviated, a process which results in various forms of mental disorder or abnormality. The principle of deviations from normal growth is generally acknowledged in the vegetable and animal world, and also in the development of the human body because, in these cases, deviations from normal growth are usually visible and hence easily recognized. But effects of misdirected mental energies (which should have gone into normal growth) are not easily recognized, partly because they are not so visibly manifest and partly because we have not as yet, as a race, even become aware of the traits of normal mental development, since abnormalities are so universal.

These deviations from normal mental growth take on many and different forms in childhood. Disobedience, rebellion, tantrums, lying and other forms of deceit, greediness in food, nightmares, bed wetting, extreme possessiveness — these are some of them and there are many more. There are other forms of deviation which, strange to say, are often thought of as attractive characteristics of childhood. Such, for instance, include an extreme dependence on or attachment to some other person. Again, such a high degree of imaginative development as to cause the child to live in an imaginary world of his own creation is really a form of deviation, though certain grownups often praise it. ("He has such a wonderful imagination," they say admiringly.) Again it is almost universally believed that children prefer play to work. Many persons think it is not natural for free children to be anything else than rowdy or boisterous. Likewise they think it is "against their nature" for children to sit still and concentrate spontaneously on work for long periods of time, without being forced into doing so by external influences. Yet Montessori asserts that inability to do these things is a deviation from the normal. The truly normal child loves work. He can and does concentrate on it spontaneously for long periods. Furthermore, the truly normal child is not possessive with regard to the objects in his environment. He loves order and is careful of property. He is helpful to others and manifests a high degree of self-discipline.

How does Montessori come to make these assertions? What grounds has she for drawing this new picture of the normal child? The answer is quite simple. She has seen it herself. And thousands of her followers have seen it with her.

When children are treated in such a way that their (biological) independence is respected, when they are placed in an environment specially corresponding to their needs, both physical and mental, when they are given accurate and detailed instruction on how to carry out the various orderly occupations in this environment, and above all, when they are given freedom to choose their occupations and to work at them for as long as they like, undisturbed by adult intervention — in a word, when they are given the liberty to live their own lives according to the laws of development within them, in a specially prepared environment, they then reveal themselves as different and higher beings.

This realization of the true nature of the normalized child is Montessori's great discovery and forms, at the same time, her chief claim on the gratitude of the human race. When children are so treated, after a shorter or longer time, their deviations fall away from them; they simply disappear, slough off as a snake discards its old skin. Then we see children for what they really are — lovers of work, of silence, of order, capable of continued intellectual concentration, able to choose what is good for them, serene and self-disciplined. New and higher social qualities appear also. For example, the love of possession, so common in children, vanishes to such a degree that Montessori says the motto which would best describe the attitude of these children to the material things in their environment, would be *usare sed non possedere* (to use but not to possess). Further they abandon the competitive spirit, substituting for it the principle of mutual aid.

NORMALIZATION THROUGH WORK
This change in the children's character which takes place as they settle down to the regular activities of the Montes-

sori school is summed up in Dr. Montessori's doctrine of normalization through work.

So true is this doctrine that the first thing a Montessori directress looks for in a new pupil is not whether he is getting along satisfactorily with his arithmetic or his writing or reading, but whether his character is becoming normalized. Is the newcomer beginning to slough off those various deviations such as inability to concentrate, interfering with other children, misuse of apparatus and other similar forms of disorder? For these are not the child's true self; they are but a mask hiding the real and normal child beneath. The directress is looking and waiting for the day on which this deviated child will settle down spontaneously to some occupation which he has chosen for himself, and begin to work at it with continued concentration. From the moment this happens, his feet are on the path which leads to normality and self-discipline. Day by day, in the exact degree in which he so works and concentrates spontaneously, his deviations begin to disappear. We see his character changing visibly before our eyes, until, in a shorter or longer time according to circumstances, the higher qualities above mentioned begin to reveal themselves; until, in fact, he has completed the process of normalization through work.

HOW LIBERTY IS RELATED TO LAW

Thus we see that Montessori liberty does not mean, as so many persons still falsely imagine, giving the child freedom to do anything he likes. That would be "to abandon the child, not to give him freedom." Montessori's is a disciplined freedom which leads to reality. We have it on the highest authority that "the truth shall make you free," not just thinking or believing anything you like. The control of error must always be present in the child's environment as a necessary counterpart of the liberty we grant them.

Speaking generally, we might say that, with Montessori, children are free to do what is right, but not what is wrong, nor even what is imperfect. "Never be afraid," say Montessori, "to destroy what is evil; but on the other hand you must be careful, very careful, not to destroy what is good. Every spontaneous activity of the child which is good and creative should be encouraged."

It is by no means always easy to distinguish "the wheat from the tares"—and considerable tact and experience are needed to be able to tell at a glance which actions are to be suppressed and which encouraged. Weeds and garden flowers look very similar in their early stages. It should be borne in mind, too, that in the Montessori class the liberty of the individual must not be allowed to interfere with the general good. Definitely antisocial actions are always to be discouraged. "The liberty of the individual has as its limit the collective interest."

It will be evident, from what we have written, that at the beginning, when the children have learned nothing, neither how to perform the exercises of practical life nor how to work even with the sensorial materials, there will necessarily be much less individual liberty in the class and much more direct control by the directress. It is only gradually that true freedom appears or can appear. It is, in fact, only in proportion as the children acquire *first*, independence—i.e., the capacity to act alone—and, *secondly*, the knowledge of how to use the various materials, that they are sufficiently prepared to be able to enjoy liberty in the schoolroom. Before this state has been reached, it would be impossible for the teacher to *give* them true liberty, even if she wanted to—they could not take it!

It will be seen more clearly, now, how indispensable a factor is the presence of the prepared environment, with all its purposeful activities, in making it possible for us to grant liberty to the children. It would certainly not be granting a true liberty, in the Montessori sense, if one were to say to children in an ordinary classroom (unfurnished with the immense variety of occupations which are found in a Montessori schoolroom): "Now, children, you are free to choose your own work."

Biologically speaking, there is a certain relationship between any organism and the factors it requires in its environment in order that it may carry on its life freely and satisfactorily. The more complicated the organism, the more factors are necessary in the environment that it may grow and function normally. Thus, for example, an environment which contained all that was necessary for the free development of plant life—sunshine, air, good soil, moisture, etc.—would not suffice for a dog. He would need, in addition, the opportunity and means to liberty of movement in order to seek his food and his mate. Again, an environment which contained sufficient elements to provide free development for a dog, or even a chimpanzee, would not suffice for the kind of liberty children need. They are "rational animals" and therefore require, in addition, factors in their environment which answer to the needs, not only of their vegetable and animal functions, but to their intellectual, social and spiritual natures as well.

Finally, we may add that, whatever may be one's theory as to the nature of liberty, one interesting and important fact stands out as incontrovertible. It is that, in the Montessori classroom, liberty and self-discipline go hand in hand. Indeed we might say they are aspects of the same thing, like the two sides of a coin. If there were no liberty, there would never come into existence that wonderful self-discipline which is perhaps the most astonishing of all the wonderful revelations which these new children have shown us. On the other hand, if there were no self-discipline there could be no true liberty.

THE INNER GUIDE

Why does the child choose one occupation rather than another? Who is this mysterious teacher who makes out his program for the day? And why does he obey it with such fidelity? What teacher, acting from the outside, would obtain such marvels of concentration and such exactitude? The child *"who has developed normally"* (we stress this, as it is very important) "reveals himself as being in the possession of an inner guide." This inner guide, if he has been permitted to become sensitive to its promptings, enables him to choose the work which will best assist his development, at the same time evoking an intense concentration.

It is interesting to note, says Montessori, that not every occupation undertaken by the child during the morning reveals this power of creative choice, but only that occupation which Montessori calls "the great work." A child will often select one or two occupations at the beginning of the morning, staying at each a comparatively short time—as if he were trying himself out. These form a sort of *hors d'-oeuvre* to the *chef d'oeuvre* to follow. Once he has settled down to his great work, it is of the utmost importance to let it go on uninterrupted for as long as he wants to keep at it. The child may repeat an exercise ten, twenty, or even fifty times; and we must let him do so without judging him to have had enough. He will stop as soon as his inner guide tells him to.

"This cycle of work has its beginning and ending like a day. It must be allowed to come full circle. You must not imagine that the child will weary himself. The sun rises and sets continually and is never weary. No one ever said

94

to the sun: 'Stop, you will become weary.' Similarly, these children demonstrate that if they can be allowed to finish their cycle of work they do not become weary. The only thing that tires the child is to be interrupted in the midst of his great work, because that inner master which guides him has taught him that the only way he can work without getting tired is to complete his cycle of work."

Here we have another of those mysterious inner laws (like the law of sensitive periods in development) which Montessori has discovered, or, rather, which these free children were able to reveal to her just because of their freedom. "Everyone rests when he is working according to the law of his nature"—a sentence which reminds one of St. Augustine's saying that "love is never at rest until it is at work."

This is the reason why the child, on coming to the end of his long and intense cycle of work, looks strengthened and refreshed. Since we are created for activity, "what is tiring is work done outside the laws of our nature. Inactivity is just as far from giving us rest as the wrong kind of activity."

Montessori goes farther and asserts that the whole moral nature of the child is elevated when he is allowed to complete his cycle of work. It seems to have the effect of purging his system of all sorts of moral disorders and psychic defects. We have already touched on this matter in discussing Montessori's doctrine of normalization through work. We find here the natural starting point of moral development; because it has been found that the child, so refreshed and contented after his cycle of work, often seems to be in a condition of soul or spirit especially apt to receive and respond to religious influences. This is because "he has been put in order with regard to the fundamental needs of his mental life, in a manner which could not be attained in any other way."

THE CHILD MUST BE TREATED AS AN ELEVATED BEING

The whole burden of this outline is to emphasize the fact that Montessori will go down to history as a great discoverer rather than as the founder of an educational system. We assert this because she has been the first to see and describe the characteristics of the normalized child. It is this higher type of child, usually hidden beneath the mask of deviations, which so astonished visitors to the first Montessori schools that they found themselves forced to speak in superlative terms, and to make use of such phrases as "the New Children" when describing them.

The emergence of these higher traits of character in normalized children is not only a matter of historical and psychological interest, but is a factor of great practical importance when we come to the problem of how best to transmit the elements of culture in the children in our schools.

We must never forget that the child is potentially a much higher being than we have hitherto imagined and we must always treat him as such. This means that we must present the elements of culture to him, not in any low or mechanical way, but in a manner which corresponds to this newly revealed and more elevated nature.

Let us take an example. Writing and reading are, when you consider them in their essential nature, tremendous achievements of the human race. They represent truly great discoveries in the cultural progress of mankind. Indeed they are so important that, taken together, they may be said to form the bridge or line of demarcation between prehistory and history. To those far-off ancestors of ours these accomplishments must have seemed so wonderful as to appear little short of miraculous—as they still do to primitive races .

Now, says Montessori, the small child, even the child of four and a half to five and a half, is already so elevated a being that, if we arrange things in the proper way, he will be able to recapture and relive, in his own individual development, those same wonderful discoveries made so long ago by the race. And, in so reliving and discovering them, he will experience the same raptures of discovery, and the same thrill of newly awakened powers, as did those primitive ancestors.

This same principle—that of treating the child always as an elevated being—is equally to be borne in mind in teaching all other subjects in the curriculum. We must present them in the most elevated manner possible, so as to awaken wonder and joy in these souls who are capable of so much more than we usually imagine. Those who have worked (as has the writer) in direct contact with these free children in their prepared environment never cease to wonder at the unexpected depth of their intellectual comprehension and the startling elevation of their sentiments. Again and again it is a case of *"ex ore infantium. . . ."*

The practical details of presenting the various subjects in this inspiring way belong rather to the training college than to such an introductory book as this. We are concerned only with pointing out the general principle that it is a scientifically established fact that, when we do treat these little ones as more elevated beings, they respond in a striking manner. We find them absorbing ideas and revealing sentiments which we should have imagined far beyond their years. We also find them spontaneously making discoveries in various fields of knowledge which fill us with amazement.

SOCIAL DEVELOPMENT IN THE MONTESSORI METHOD

It would not be right to conclude this outline of Montessori principles without some reference to the social development of children under Montessori's system. A criticism sometimes leveled against her method of education is that it is too individualistic. It cannot be denied that individual work is the general rule and collective teaching the exception. Yet it remains equally true that there are far more and far better opportunities for social intercourse and social development in a Montessori school than under the old system. Collective teaching, as such, does not make for social life but rather the reverse. In the ordinary schoolroom, tendencies toward the expression of the social sentiments are only too often nipped in the bud. Children are not encouraged to talk with their neighbors, still less to move about the room making further contacts. As Montessori points out: "Social life does not come into existence through mere juxtaposition." It is, rather, a group of individuals in free association, each of whom is conscious of his responsibility to the common weal.

No competent observer could spend even ten minutes in a Montessori class without becoming vividly aware that a genuine social life is going on under his eyes. As the children move about freely on their proper business in their common environment, they meet and salute each other, they discuss common problems, they correct each others' mistakes, they borrow and lend to each other, they answer queries, and they help each other in many other ways. All this is a form of social life. What is even more interesting is the fact that it often happens that a number of children, quite spontaneously, form themselves into a group to carry out some task in unison. At these times an even higher form of social life comes into existence, one which involves a real division of labor. Such collective enterprises may take the form of one of the exercises of practical life, such as preparing a meal, setting a table, or washing up. At other times a group may be formed to carry out some complicated operation of arithmetic, such as long multiplication with the bank material. One child will calculate the multiples, another will act as banker, while a third manipulates the trays and organizes the numbers placed in them—each thus performing a different but essential part of the operation, the final result being a genuine collective achievement.

We have already pointed out that it is a constant feature of a Montessori school that more advanced children spontaneously help their less developed neighbors, which in itself is a most valuable social training. So far, then, from it being true that the Montessori system tends to make children so isolated as to be antisocial in its effect, the very opposite is true. In every good Montessori class we see a real social life which develops, quite naturally and spontaneously, from moment to moment and day to day.

LESSONS OF GRACE AND COURTESY

Here, in this question of social training and development, as always with Montessori, it is our duty to second nature. That is why from the very beginning, indeed especially at the beginning and with the smaller children, the directress spends a good deal of time presenting what Montessori calls the lessons in grace and courtesy. These include definite and detailed instructions on such matters as how to salute another properly, how and when to apologize for disturbing or inconveniencing another, how to hand objects to another, especially such things as knives, scissors, etc., how to wait at table, how to sit down and stand up correctly, how to welcome a visitor and offer him a chair, and a hundred other such actions. All of these help toward the smooth running of social life as oil does a machine. In teaching these lessons of grace and courtesy, as with almost everything taught in a Montessori school, there are two stages. The first is a comparatively short one consisting of a presentation by the directress. The second and more important stage consists in the freely chosen and spontaneous repetition of the action. This stage may go on at intervals for days, or even weeks, until the lesson sinks into the child's very self and becomes a part of him.

Montessori urges the importance of giving these lessons in grace and courtesy at an early age (four to six years), for at this stage of their development the children are passing through a sensitive period characterized by a special capacity for fixing sensory-motor activities of this kind, thus making them habitual. All this amounts to saying that there is a special period in a child's life when he is most apt to pick up good manners. Consequently, if presented at this epoch, we see the children in the *casa dei bambini* acquiring these social accomplishments with ease and joy. Whereas, if it is left to a later period, it is much more difficult to make them learn such things, since by that time this particular sensitive period has passed away— and for ever.

Speaking generally, we might say that, in the Montessori infants class and the earlier stages of the elementary school age, emphasis is laid upon the more external aspects of social life, i.e., good manners and etiquette. At a later stage of development social training takes on a deeper and more inward or moral character. During this period the sense of social responsibility can be best helped by means of special youth organizations. The aim of such groups (which, of course, must be established and guided by adults) should be the refinement of conscience, and the development of the sense of duty and of moral values generally.

THE LATER STAGES OF DEVELOPMENT

The boy or girl at this stage (eight to twelve years) requires for his full sound development—for the valorization of his personality—to be brought into contact with a wider social environment than his family or school can provide.

According to Montessori, the Boy Scout (and Girl Scout) movement provides, in many ways, a better response to the social and moral needs of this stage than does the ordinary school. Here again, however, it must be remembered that social life does not come into existence by a number of persons simply living together like animals in a herd. Not the walls of a building, but a common aim, the aspiration to a higher and more difficult moral standard than prevails outside—this is what should form the true limits to the group at this stage.

In the final epoch of the individual's development, that of adolesence, the question of social training and the right adjustment of the individual to society becomes even more important. In fact, according to Montessori, it becomes a matter of such paramount importance at this stage that it should take precedence over all other claims—even those of scholarship.

To explain this subject fully would, however, involve us in a discussion on the whole question of secondary education as Montessori sees it; and this cannot be attempted on account of the limits we have set ourselves.

All we can say here is that Montessori had very definite ideas as to the urgent necessity of reform in secondary education, and also as to the means of bringing it about. To a certain degree, however, this question of the reform of secondary education according to Montessori principles is still a matter for the future. For, although Montessori has clearly laid down the principles which should guide us in dealing with the development of the adolescent, they have never yet been fully and completely put into practice as she would have them carried out. Furthermore, she admits that the working out of the details of any such scheme would necessarily be gradual. Such a development could, in fact, come to complete fruition only as these principles become gradually incarnated in a living adolescent society —an achievement which would involve much labor, collaboration and experimental research.

THE NEW CHILDREN

On the other hand, all the other phenomena which we have been describing—those that pertain to the ages from birth to ten years—are scientifically established beyond question. They are matters of history and science which cannot be denied.

The New Child is not a figment of the imagination, nor just a pious hope. He is a scientific fact, which—like all other scientific facts—is capable of verification, in any country at any time, by any person or group of persons who will take the trouble to prepare the right conditions, and bring them together in the right proportions. Given the new teacher, i.e., the Montessori directress with her entirely different approach—*and* the prepared environment —then, as surely as day follows night, you will see the emergence of what, for want of a better term, we call the New Children.

PART TWO
MONTESSORI ILLUSTRATED

The Montessori materials are often called the didactic or teaching materials, but their more accurate name would be the materials for development. Each of the sensorial materials is, in fact, a series of objects with which the child carries out a definite piece of work, which assists and directs the development of his personality.

This explains why the child repeats and repeats these exercises so many times, for subconsciously he feels that each repetition promotes inward growth. At this early stage he is especially interested in any material which evokes a concentration of his attention combined with an activity which develops and refines his sensorial perceptions.

Later, when his reasoning powers have awakened, the materials for development direct the child along cultural paths through co-operation between the senses and the intellect.

CHAPTER THREE

FROM THE BROOM TO BINOMIAL THEOREMS

THE IMMENSE CONTRIBUTION OF MONTESSORI to education has been the way she leads the child (aged about three) from the simplest exercises in muscular co-ordination (walking a chalk line), via the Exercises of Practical Life (scrubbing tables, pouring something from one container into another, sweeping the floor), into learning to read and write through the sensory-motor material which, easily but progressively, leads him to the most abstract sort of calculation—fractions, square root, musical composition, theology and archaeology.

It begins and ends with the magic shelves where all these fascinating and creative tools are kept. In a class of thirty to forty children, one or two are nearly always at the shelves. They have finished one occupation and, after replacing the material, select another. This is an essential part of the prepared environment.

In Part One we have tried to give our readers a quick bird's-eye view of the theory behind the Montessori Method (which has been analyzed at greater length in *Maria Montessori: Her Life And Work*; and which will be developed more philosophically in future books). In Part Three we have attempted to show the theory in practice—by actual on-the-scene observation.

And yet, *this* is the heart of the book. The Chinese say that "One picture is worth a thousand words." Montessori, who depended so much on visual as well as auditory and kinesthetic aids, would agree. Besides, we have here the most fascinating and unselfconscious models the world can provide. (I am sorry that in this selection of photographs, which I have collected over many years and in many countries—England, Holland, Italy, Ireland, Spain, India, Germany, Africa and now America—I cannot remember the various photographers, often amateur, whom I should credit. I hope they will forgive me.)

THE CHILDREN'S HOUSE

The key word, of course, is the prepared environment—a situation in which the child's needs and dimensions govern, and not the grownups'. The Montessori school is essentially—and first of all—a place in which a child can feel at home, and work according to his own tempo and ability. Everything is scaled to his size, within his own reach—and, preferably, as the Hemingway short story was titled, "A Clean, Well-Lighted Place." (Of course, Mr. Hemingway was being ironic. His story is an indictment of what is wrong with adults produced by our usual unfeeling, haphazard education.)

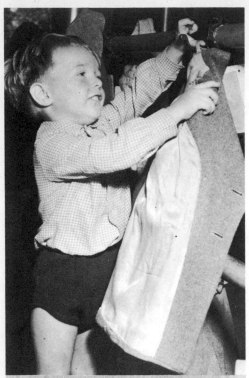

I like hanging up my coat by myself—that is, if you give me a conveniently low peg, and plenty of time to do it. (Acton, England.)

Note Kaaren's waterproof apron, the old-fashioned pitcher and basin which encourage her to use muscles (and care) that modern plumbers deny. Note, too, that the equipment is built for her own height and reach.

The Button Frame (U.S.A.)

Cleaning and polishing metal objects is a popular occupation in a Montessori Classroom.

Window-cleaning requires especial care and co-ordination. It is a well-paid profession for those who wash the windows of New York skyscrapers. These Dutch children take their responsibility seriously.

"Look on this picture and on that."—(HAMLET)

In the first scene, *The Infant School* by Jean Geoffroy, we see plenty of activity, it is true. But this activity is disordered, frittered away in wasteful channels, instead of being used to build up and strengthen the child's personality.

The distracted teacher, doing his best no doubt, is striving in vain—even with the help of physical force—to hold the attention of two children. He is using a visual aid, but with small children this is not enough. They need a sensory-*motor* aid. That is, they need a material which solicits a definite movement directed by the intelligence to a definite end, and which forms a point of contact between the child's mind and an external reality. Through this work with the materials, the child is acquiring new knowledge and deepening what he already knows.

Now look at Scene B. Here again we see activity, but it is ordered, definite, tranquil and sustained. The mental and physical energies of these children are working in harmony, integrated by a conjoint operation, brought about by concentration on the various teaching materials they are using. These children are calm, serene and full of a deep joy. It is the joy that Nature always gives to the right use of our God-given faculties. All the children's energies are being used constructively. Here, too, is self-discipline, which has been achieved through a spontaneous concentration on work which creates order within as well as without.

108

The Sound Boxes are all alike — except in the sounds they emit when shaken.

The Sophia School in Santa Monica, U. S.A.

ISOLATION OF SENSORY STIMULI

The first materials the beginners at a Montessori school are introduced to—the cylinders, the geometric forms, the color tablets, the bells, etc.—are calculated to teach them to match, grade and differentiate by means of all the senses.

The cylinders—the first exercise—involve putting various pegs into their appropriate holes, and call for sight and touch. Another primary introduction is the feeling of textures and shapes—with cloth, sandpaper, geometric objects (using a blindfold to separate the senses). The olfactory sense is involved when Montessori children sniff various pungent odors in order to grade them. The ear is called on when pitch is matched by the bells.

And then the aesthetic sense is developed in matching colors—and later in graduating them from dark to light.

Each of the didactic materials is calculated to appeal to the child at the primary stage of his interest—to "hook" him and carry him irresistibly through to the next stage (leaving an important residue of information behind). The hook reaches from the cylinders into writing and geometry, from the blocks of the Pink Tower and the Broad Stair into Higher Mathematics. The child who has mastered the sense of color from the color tablets will begin to paint like a Picasso; the one who has mastered pitch with the bells will begin to compose, as our friend in the illustration did.

Dr. Montessori described this primary phase as that of the "isolation of sensory stimulus."

THE COLOR TABLETS

The color tablets are the same in size, shape and weight and are made of the same kind of wood on exactly the same pattern. They differ only in their colors. Hence the mind becomes psychologically blind to all the other qualities except color, which is the attribute upon which we want the child to concentrate in these exercises. Here we see a pupil grading the different shades of each color from the darkest to the lightest.

111

Here we see a child doing another sensory exercise based on the sense of color, pairing or matching *identical* colors. First of all, the color tablets are mixed up, higgledy-piggledy, on the table. Then the child picks up a color at random and looks for its mate. Once having found it, she puts the two reds, or greens, or whatever it may be, down on the table together forming an orderly pattern. As usual with Montessori, we see order coming out of chaos. The isolation of the color stimulus makes the exercise easy and pleasant. This child is at the sensitive period for sensory refinement.

THE BELLS

All the bells are exactly the same size and shape, like silver mushrooms on brown stalks. The only way they can be distinguished and arranged in pairs or in a graded scale is by their pitch. The little girl is doing this by striking each bell with a small hammer and comparing the pitch as a basis for classification. In her left hand is a flat piece of wood with a felt pad on one end. This is to stop the vibration of the bell when she is ready to pass on to the next one.

THE BELLS AS A MUSICAL INSTRUMENT

The bells have also a higher function than a mere sensory exer-cise. When arranged in a scale they can be used for learning the names of the notes and for playing tunes. This illustration shows a small boy playing a tune which he composed himself to go with one of his favorite poems from "A Child's Garden of Verses" by Robert Louis Stevenson. (*Photo taken at a school in Acton, England.*)

KNOWLEDGE AT A PRIMARY STAGE

The important thing to remember is that, even at this primary stage, habits are being developed which will lead the child into his next "explosion." He has, for example, been using his writing fingers to manipulate the cylinders and has been writing in parallel strokes when he colored his insets.

It is the same with many other subjects. The children in these photographs are making a real botanical study of leaf forms (largely on a sensorial level) and are also learning their classification and nomenclature.

Cards with leaf forms painted on them are placed on a table in the garden. The child chooses a card and then wanders through the garden trying to find a leaf form on some living plant to correspond with that on the card. It is great fun — rather like a treasure hunt and a lesson combined. Nonetheless, it is a real study and will form the basis of a deeper study later on.

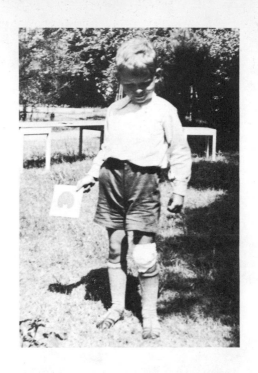

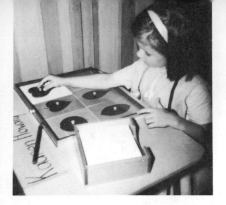 

ISOLATION OF DIFFICULTIES

The sense of touch is more important to young children than to older ones or to adults. Little children are always touching things in response to a natural urge. Montessori makes educational use of this instinct as a preparation for writing.

Learning Celtic Letters in Ireland.

One of her applications is in learning the shapes of the letters and how to make them. The letters of the alphabet are cut from sandpaper and pasted on stiff cardboard mounts. At this early age, the children love to trace over the letters with the first and second fingers of the right hand — the writing fingers — while at the same time they pronounce the phonetic sound of the letter. *If this is done at the right epoch*, a child will learn to make all the letters in about six weeks. By repetition the child acquires a stereognostic memory of the letters, i.e., a sort of muscular memory at the same time as a visual one.

Sensory exercise in graded dimensions.
(A Montessori school in Bengal.)

If the child is also doing parallel exercises (such as composing words with the movable alphabet), there will soon occur the phenomenon of the "explosion into writing."

But this *must* be done at the right age, before the sensitive period for touch has vanished, never to return. It would be useless to give the sandpaper letters to a boy of ten who could not write, for he would have no interest in tracing the letters. Yet a child of four and a half will often spontaneously trace the letters ten or twenty, or even fifty, times.

This is an example of a particular difficulty isolated and dealt with through an activity of intrinsic, though transient, interest.

PREPARATION FOR THE EXPLOSION INTO WRITING

One of the difficulties in learning to write is acquiring the ability to hold a pencil properly and to control its movements. With Montessori, this skill is acquired by means of a separate exercise, which is not writing but preparation for it.

This is an interesting occupation which consists in tracing designs made with the metal insets, used singly or in combination, and then filling them in carefully and evenly with parallel lines made with colored crayons. Besides teaching the child to control the writing instrument, it also develops a sense of the harmony of colors and is, in fact, a form of decorative art.

In writing a word or sentence, you must think of many things at the same time if you are a beginner — the shape of the letters, making them with the hand, holding the pencil, and also the spelling. This last difficulty is tackled in isolation by the composition of words with the movable script letters.

In phonetic languages, such as German and Italian, children can and do compose quite astonishingly long words. They already know the shapes and sounds of the letters and they simply analyze the component phonetic sounds of the words and put down the corresponding letters — and presto! the word is there. This exercise is easier and more interesting because the children are still in the sensitive period for language.

Making up words and sentences with the movable letters. She is an Irish lassie, as one could tell from the use of the word "bold" (mischievous). Taken in a Dublin Montessori school. Here again is spontaneous concentration on real work.

This is not writing and it is not reading which the child cannot yet do. What is it then? Composing words with the movable alphabet, after first analyzing their component sounds—psychologically a very different thing; for the child very often cannot read the words she herself composed ten minutes before.

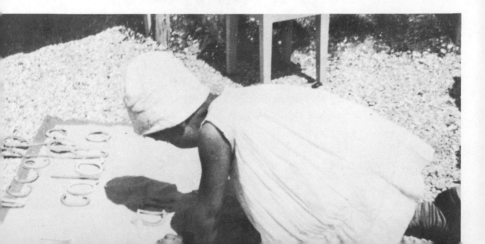

This boy is working with one of the grammar boxes mentioned in the text. All the words of one part of speech, e.g., the verbs, are written on slips of paper of the same color and kept in one of the divisions in the grammar box.

GEOMETRY: ANOTHER EXPLOSION

In most schools geometry is an advanced subject — one reserved for students who have a certain capacity for abstraction and intellectual concepts. The *Dottoressa* discovered, on the other hand, that the youngest children — with their special sensitivity to shapes — can most easily grasp the implications of Euclid.

Plato wrote over the entrance to his Academy: "Let no one ignorant of geometry enter here." It would very much have surprised the learned philosopher if one fine day a group of Montessori children with their shining morning faces had passed through that portal. And if Plato, pointing to the inscription (which many of them could read), had begun to shoo them like chickens from the porch, the children might well and truly have replied: "But we are *not* ignorant of geometry! The top of that wine beaker is a circle, so is the sun and so is that plate. Your room is a rectangle, that table is square and that pediment on the temple over there is a triangle."

What Plato did not realize is that one can have knowledge of a subject on different levels. *He* thought of geometry in terms of syllogisms — given certain data, certain things must logically follow — "Q.E.D." and all that. This, of course, was an excellent preparation for the dialectic discussions which he and Socrates and the rest delighted in.

But the fact remains that these children have a real knowledge of geometric forms, although it is on a sensorial level, and of geometric nomenclature also, for they are still at the sensitive period for language.

As a matter of fact, the knowledge of these children is closely akin to the original geometry which arose in Egypt and which simply meant the measurement of land.

ASSISTING NATURE

It is as natural for a child's mind to make abstractions as it is for a bird to fly. In this picture we see some of the materials for sensorial geometry.

They vary from the geometrical forms on the left, passing through intermediate stages in which matter is less and less in evidence, until we come to the forms shown only by a thin line.

There is a further stage, but it must be accomplished in the mind. It is the last stage, the mental creation of the abstract idea of the circle or rectangle or whatever it may be.

We see here, typically, an example of the way Montessori always assists nature to do, more easily and more perfectly, what she will in any case attempt to do by herself.

Between this sensorial geometry and the Euclidean geometry, Montessori has an intermediate stage, the advanced Montessori material, in working with which the child's reason comes ever more to the fore as the purely sensorial impressions correspondingly recede.

The study of geometric forms begins early at a sensorial level. The children are replacing the cut-out wooden forms (regular polygons) in their respective sockets — the boy above by the sense of sight, the girl below by the sense of touch.

The Number Rods

"OLD FRIENDS AGAIN"

According to the principle of the hook, each Montessori material, besides having a present interest and function, leads on to something in the future.

These children, about three and a half years of age, are absorbed in a sensorial exercise (almost the first they can do) which is based on a study of the comparative sizes of objects in a series. (These objects differ in three dimensions, the Long Stair only in one dimension.) When properly completed, the child has built the Pink Tower.

Months or years later, when he studies the decimal system, he will learn that the largest cube is a thousand times as large as the smallest one. The base of the Tower has a volume of one liter and the smallest block is one cubic centimeter.

The latter, if filled with water at four degrees centigrade, would equal one gram — the unit of weight.

Thus he would find his old friends again, but on a different level. Similarly, he would learn that the longest number rod (and the red rod) are both one meter in length, and the smallest is one decimeter.

The Pink Tower (U.S.A.)

The Pink Tower (Ceylon)

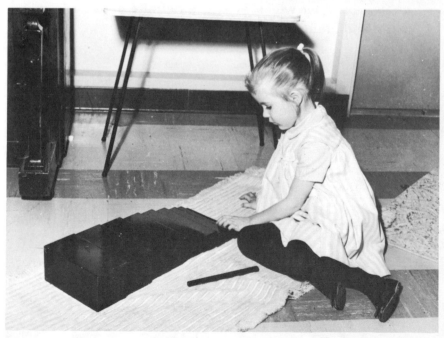

The Broad Stair (U.S.A.)

KNOWLEDGE AT SEVERAL LEVELS
*"One lesson, nature, let me learn of thee
Of toil unsevered from tranquillity."*—Wordsworth

If one looks at these two pictures, they appear, superficially, to be very much the same — just a boy putting out some beads on a table. But a deeper understanding will show much more than this.

1. The boy is *working* — doing a real intellectual operation — not playing. He is making a study of the numbers 10 to 19 by composing them with notation cards and the corresponding beads — units and tens.

2. He is *working by himself*, independently. Indeed he was scarcely conscious of the photographer because

3. He is *exceptionally concentrated on his work* and it is spontaneous concentration, inspired by no extrinsic interest such as marks, fear of punishment, or competition.

4. The reason for this concentration is that he is *working with a material* which evokes a definite activity in which hand and brain work together.

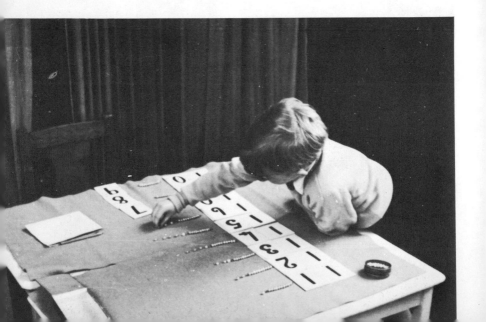

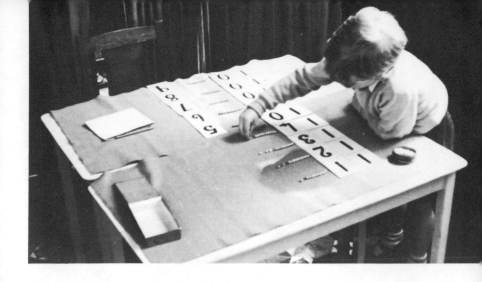

5. It is real *autoeducation,* for he is teaching himself by means of the material and the activity. At the end he will know much more than he did at the beginning.

6. He is *working at his own rhythm.* Hence there is no sense of hurry or fatigue.

7. Actually (although you cannot tell this from the picture) he has *chosen this particular work* from a great variety of other occupations, and it was chosen because he already knew enough about it to be interested. He chose from knowledge, not mere curiosity.

*Assigning cards to the number rods
before adding.*

Making the numbers 10 to 19 with the "Hymn Board" material. (England)

Adding by placing two number rods end to end and counting along both of them.

One of the most valuable conditions for acquiring new knowledge *spontaneously* consists in spreading out the knowledge we have already acquired and then, as it were, rising above it and seeing it all from a new and different angle of vision. In this way one may come to see new and unexpected relationships.

To take an example: In most nursery schools the children of four to five, who are beginning numbers, occupy themselves for a considerable time with numerical operations on a very small scale (e.g., $5 + 9 = 14$). But with Montessori, thanks to the invention of the golden bead decimal system of concrete numbers, the child who can count up to ten is at once introduced to tens, hundreds, and even thousands. It is in fact just as easy to put out six thousand-bead cubes as six unit beads — easier, in fact, for the unit beads are mobile little fellows and are inclined to run about on their own, whereas the thousand-bead cubes stand solidly and majestically firm in their shining splendor.

In the picture the child is putting out the bird's eye view of the decimal system, with number cards up to 9,000 and beads to correspond.

When it is all finished, she will stand back and survey the work of her hands from above in a sort of three-dimensional way. She will observe (or perhaps the teacher will help her by asking questions) that in each column of symbolic numbers, there are just the same figures — 1, 2, 3, 4, 5, 6, 7, 8, 9. Always the same row of figures, *ending* at *nine* — "at nine there is always a crisis"). This 1, 2, 3, 4, 5, 6, 7, 8, 9 is like a refrain that occurs again and again, in different keys but always to the same melody.

THE FOURTH DIMENSION?

Even an adult can discover from this material, so spread out, things he did not realize before. You will notice that the first member of the unit column is just a single unit bead — like a point in space with no dimension. The first in the ten column (the ten-bead bar) is a straight line which has one dimension. The first in the hundred column is a square, which has two dimensions — length and breadth. The first in the thousand column is a cube, with three dimensions — length, breadth and height.

Immediately the mind wonders what will happen if the process is carried still further. Shall we come to the fourth dimension at last? And, if not, why not? Without answering the problem we can point out something typical of the Montessori materials, viz., that they are invitations, summoning the children to further research.

Then again, how clearly one sees the function of the zeros. The units have none, the tens have one, the hundreds two and the thousands three.

The next stage, which follows naturally, is *the composition of numbers* — big numbers, as big as the license number on Daddy's car. Here, in an Indian Montessori school at Hyderabad, we see a little girl busy composing the number 5,764 with the cards and the beads.

It is only a step now to doing the four operations in arithmetic with the big numbers. All we must remember is that "when we come to nine there is always a crisis" and, if we get more than nine we must go to the bank and change our beads for members in the next section of the hierarchy of numbers. It is quite simple and great fun, especially when we work in a group and one of us acts as banker.

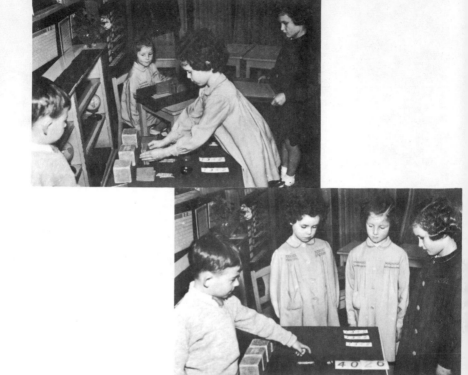

MULTIPLICATION

These children are doing a multiplication exercise as a group (1,342 x 3). Each of the three little girls has brought the number 1,342, in concrete materials, on a tray and placed it on the table with corresponding number cards.

Then the little boy, who is the Master of Ceremonies, has added them. In so doing he has gone to the bank twice, once to change ten tens for a hundred, and once to change ten hundreds for a thousand. The answer is 4,026.

It is clearly seen that the essence of multiplication is addition in equal quantities. Later on, of course, they will use multiplication tables, which are like seven league boots, and enable one to arrive at the desired end much more swiftly — "almost as if you were flying."

Long Division in the Concrete

This child is dividing a number by 231.
The cubes are thousands, the lines are
ten-bead bars, the dots are units. Do
you understand why you "subtract and
bring down the next figure?" She does.

Long Division (Nigeria)

Study of the Squares and Cubes of the numbers 1 to 10

These two young mathematicians (in Rome) are doing sums with the golden bead decimal system. On the slate is written: 1213 + *and they are*
591

working it out in the concrete. All the four operations of arithmetic can be done with this material, as well as many other problems (e.g., square root).

Finding the Square Root by means of symbolic pegs and peg board.

KNOWLEDGE AT DIFFERENT LEVELS: FRACTIONS

This child, aged five, is doing fractions, but in her own way and according to her degree of mental development. She can count to ten and is working with the divided circles. She knows that 1/4 means one broken into four equal parts and one taken, and so on with the other fractions. She is putting little labels on each divided circle—two 1/2 labels on one, three 1/3 labels on another, up to the circle divided into ten equal parts. She knows what a numerator and denominator *are*, although she does not know them by those terms.

140

Another child, a year or two older, is working with the same materials, but on a higher plane. She is taking 1/2, 1/3 and 1/6 and is going to add them together. To do this, she will have to "make change" to bring them to the same denominator, turning them all into sixths.

This picture shows a further stage. The girl on the left is doing more advanced sums with fractions. The apparatus on the table is used to teach how to divide by a fraction.

A STUDY OF THE CHRISTIAN YEAR

The big circle on the ground represents the liturgical year, and is divided into six sections—Advent, Christmastide, and so on. It is further subdivided into 52 parts, being the Sundays of the year. These children have just finished putting out labels on each of which is written one of the Sundays of the year, e.g., the third Sunday in Lent, the first Sunday in Advent and so on.

PART THREE
MONTESSORI IN ACTION

*Doctor Montessori often used to express herself as fol-
lows: "I give lectures and write books, and have done so
for years, but that does not spread my method. It is the
children themselves who spread it. People think that I
am exaggerating when I tell them about all the wonderful
things that are done in my schools by the New Children,
as they have often been called. But one fine day they
decide to go and visit a genuine Montessori school for
themselves, and then they are convinced."*

*That is the reason why we have devoted a section
of this book to a description of what we have actually
seen and heard ourselves in various Montessori schools
in different countries.*

*But there is nothing special about these descriptions. The
same sort of things are going on NOW in a score of different
countries all over the world and can be seen by those who
will take the trouble to look for them in the right places.*

INTRODUCTION

MOST OF THE INCIDENTS DESCRIBED IN THIS CHAPTER were recorded during a series of not more than a dozen visits to various Montessori schools in England made during one of Dr. Montessori's training courses. These observations were jotted down without embellishment just as they happened. That is their merit, for, to those who read them with discernment, they should make clear that a Montessori school is essentially a place where things are constantly happening. According to Montessori's own definition, it is a place where children "can live their own lives freely, according to the laws of development within them, undisturbed by adult intervention." The charm and wonder of a Montessori school lies in the fact that it is a place where the unexpected is always taking place.

Every day, every hour, indeed every moment, the unforeseen occurs. That is why the life of the Montessori directress is so different, so much more interesting—not to say exciting—than that of an ordinary teacher. For her, no less than for the children, every new day as it comes is a fresh adventure, because neither she nor they know what is going to happen.

The reactions of living beings, even the lowest, are never wholly predictable, and the higher we rise in the scale of being the more unforeseen they become. Hence the life of the free child in the prepared environment of the Montessori school is a continuously new creation, like a work of art. Indeed it may justly be compared to a work of art and each child to a genius at work on a masterpiece. For it is through the "work" of the child, more than anything else, that nature achieves her greatest masterpiece—man.

A PASSION FOR COUNTING

Many of the children, especially the smaller ones (about four years of age), show a spontaneous passion for counting which reveals itself in many ways. One little fellow was doing an exercise which consisted in simply laying out a row of cards on the table, with the numbers 1, 2, 3, 4, etc., up to ten written on them, and then putting out underneath the corresponding number of colored discs, arranging them as he did so in a pattern so that one could see the difference between the odds and evens.

Another little child, who had taken a packet of reading commands from the cupboard, was carefully counting them through, although no one had suggested that she do so. She did it simply from the desire to count.

Another day I was watching an older child making up addition sums by placing a number of variously colored bead bars in a line end to end. She wrote the numbers down on a piece of paper, thus 6 4 3 7 9 3 8 = and then, with the help of the corresponding bead bars, added up the whole series. This was the recognized way of using the particular beads. But an unexpected innovation followed. A smaller girl, who was still only at the stage of learning to count up to ten, was sitting by her at the same table, and, while the elder girl added up the row of numbers to get the sum of the whole series, the little one, simply regarding the various bars as a set of similar objects, counted their number as such. So while the answer to the older girl's sum was forty, that of her little friend was seven (i.e., seven objects).

CLIMBING THE NUMBER STAIR

When children come to the stage in which they show an interest in numbers, they are introduced to the number rods. From these they get their first clear ideas of the subject. They consist of ten rods of varying lengths, each rod representing a number from one to ten. The first exercise usually consists in laying out the rods in their proper order on a rug on the floor. Then, if it has been done properly, they form a sort of stair. I watched one little child who was busy with this material. First she took any one of the rods in her hand—the three for instance—and counted it very carefully along its divisions, "one-two-three." She went through the same performance with each of the others. Later I noticed several of the other children doing the same thing. One child held the rods in turn vertically, standing on the floor, and took a great interest in seeing how high each rod came in comparison with her own body. The ten came up to her eyebrows, which impressed her greatly.

FLYING WITH NEWLY MADE WINGS

Annette had just finished learning the numbers by means of the rods. She was threading her way through the crowded room with the longest rod, held like a lance with a number card as shield.

She was going to find the directress to corroborate the fact that it was the number ten card. The directress nodded and away went Annette back toward her rug. On the way, however, she happened to pass a table where a boy was counting out the number of coins equivalent to a shilling. At once, with the sudden and exquisite delight of a newly found power, Annette stopped and, as the little boy put down coin after coin, she began to count, too. Her face radiant with joy, she counted very solemnly and intensely, nodding her head up and down as each fresh coin was placed.

It is only when children are left free that one can properly observe the spontaneous workings of the intelligence. John, aged four and a half, was occupying himself with the Pink Tower, which consists of ten cubes, varying in size from a cubic centimenter to a cube with a side ten centimeters long. He had had his first lesson with it and had succeeded in building it up properly by himself. Three or four times in succession he ran his fingers gently up and down one side of the tower. As he did this the fourth time, the tiny cube at the top fell off. He picked it up and then, beginning at the bottom, counted all the way up from the bottom to the top, where he placed the little cube once more in position. This seemed to set going a new idea in his mind.

Now he began again counting from the bottom upwards, from one to ten, but this time on coming to the top he picked off the little cube and put it down on the rug. Again, beginning at the bottom, he counted up until he came to the ninth, which was now at the top. On coming to this, he removed it also. Then, once more, beginning at the bottom he counted up to the top again and removed the eighth cube. And so on from one to seven and one to six. At this point I noticed that he picked off the fifth cube without counting from the bottom as he had done with the previous ones. This appeared to him to be not quite playing the game. And so he put it back again and counted carefully as before from the bottom and then removed the fifth cube. And so he proceeded with the one to four and one to three. At two he again took off the top one without counting from the bottom. He again put it back, following this mysterious self-imposed rule, and once more counted from the bottom before he took away the two cube. Exactly why he made himself do it this way is hard to say, but at any rate it was an exercise of the intelligence. A dog or a monkey would never have done such a thing in a thousand years.

The other day I saw an advertisement for a public lecture to be given on the subject "Is Work Natural?" I do not know to what conclusion the lecturer came, for I was unable to attend. But I could not help thinking of his query when I saw what happened this morning.

At 11:15 a.m. the directress said: "Will you please stop working and put your things away?" She said it *three times,* each time with increasing emphasis, and yet I saw three or four of these tiny tots still working away, quite unconscious of these urgent appeals. It was a striking example of a concentration so complete that, to use Dr. Montessori's phrase, it isolates a child from his environment.

Once I came to visit a Montessori school and the teacher was late. She arrived at 2:15 p.m. instead of 2 p.m. In the meantime the children had come in, about forty of them, age five to seven. They went quietly to the cupboards and took out their various employments. By the time the teacher arrived, they were all at work except four of them, who were having a game on the floor. But the disorder from these four did not spread to the rest of the class in the infectious way that generally happens in an ordinary schoolroom.

Not long ago I was taking some students to visit another Montessori school and the teacher came rushing up in a flurry, apologizing for being a quarter of an hour late. "It was the best thing you could have done," I replied. I said this because exactly the same thing had happened, to the astonishment and admiration of the students. The children had come in, chosen their work and were quietly getting on with it, just as if the teacher had been there.

On one occasion in another school in Spain, the teacher had forgotten to bring the key to the schoolroom. But the children climbed in through a small window which was open, and settled down to their work, while the teacher remained outside until someone brought the key.

THE ROLE OF THE DIRECTRESS

Freddy had been doing the number exercises with the colored discs, and, having finished, went to the cupboard to put the material away. He next got out a reading exercise with objects and cards. This was too difficult for him, and so he gave it up after the first attempt and put it away again. This time he got nothing out of the cupboard but went wandering about the room listlessly watching the other children. Suddenly I saw the directress with him. She stooped down and whispered something in his ear. He returned to the cupboard once more, and in two minutes he was quietly at work at something else in a far corner of the room.

THE SATISFACTION OF SUCCESS

One little fellow, about four and a half years old, had been putting out the colored discs under the ciphers. When he had finished the exercise he asked the boy in front of him if they were correct. The latter turned around, surveyed it a moment and then nodded. Thereupon the little boy, who had just finished his work, lay back gazing at it, crooning to himself with great satisfaction.

The same day I noticed a boy, still younger, who was busy with the Pink Tower. He had built it up all save the last cube. Holding this in his hand he counted with it slowly from the bottom, 1, 2, 3, 4, . . . up to 10. As he said

"ten," he placed the last and smallest cube on the summit—
a really difficult feat—and, as he did so, a sudden light
flashed over his face as though he could hardly contain his
joy at having done it properly.

RELAXATION AFTER WORK

I saw a little girl working with eager delight and the utmost concentration with the sandpaper letters. One after
the other she went through them, touching them with the
tips of her writing fingers and saying their sounds aloud,
until they were all spread out on the table. For more than
an hour she had remained riveted to this occupation (quite
voluntarily, of course) and had never spoken a word, nor
got up from her place nor moved about.

I was not in the least surprised when, after this really
stupendous effort of concentration for so small a child, she
did not immediately start on any other occupation. She
simply took a chair and placed it not far away by the wall
and quietly sat there. Every now and then she would
jump down from the chair and skip and dance a little all
by herself, and then come back to sit contentedly on the
chair again. She was not aware that I was looking at her.
Mary obviously felt the need for physical and mental re-
laxation after such a prolonged effort. She played about
doing these natural gymnastics, not interfering with anyone or making any noise, and was just as happy and spontaneous in her bodily activity as before she had been in her
mental activity. Under the old methods she would have
had neither the opportunity for such a prolonged concentration nor the freedom to relax after it.

TRAINING THE WILL

One little fellow had been working on a rug on the floor.
After putting away the apparatus he had been using, he

returned, rolled up the rug carefully, and went off with it to the far end of the room to place it on the mantel shelf where it was kept. The mantel was rather high and already several rugs were on it. He was too short to reach up, so he gave the rug a little toss; but, because the other rugs placed on top of each other made a rather sloping surface, it came tumbling down again. After three unsuccessful attempts, he seemed to think the task was beyond him. So he turned and walked about the room rather vaguely looking for help. No one, however, neither child nor directress, became aware of his dilemma. And so, after waiting a minute or two, he turned back and tried once more. And again the rug rolled back on him—twice! Finally, at the sixth attempt, it stayed in place. It was a great triumph. He continued to look at it for a minute or two, half expecting it to roll down after all. Then, realizing that he had finally succeeded, he marched off with every sign of satisfaction.

This may seem a trivial incident, but little problems like this are constantly presenting themselves to these free children and calling forth decisive actions. They profit by making such acts of will, deciding for themselves what to do, in the hundred and one little emergencies of each day. Under the old system—when the children at every minute were doing what the teacher told them—it was the will of the teacher they were always carrying out. They were acting on her decisions of choice and judgment, not their own.

COURTESY AND SELF-CONTROL

It is just such repeated acts of decision that enable the will to develop by use. A little girl who had just been to the cupboard to get a button frame came with it to work at a table near where I was sitting. It happened that another girl had been working at this same table and had

151

spread out her materials on the half of it opposite her chair; but she had also left a cardboard tray on the other half of the table, opposite the empty chair. This girl chanced to be away at the moment when the newcomer arrived. The latter put down her button frame on that part of the table which was still unoccupied—a very small area indeed. She was so cramped for room, on account of the cardboard tray, that she could not get on properly with her work. Many children, finding themselves in undisputed possession of the table, would simply have moved the tray out of the way or even put it on the floor. Not so this little girl, who evinced a great respect for the absent child's work and her rights of priority.

When the other child came back again, the little newcomer asked very politely, pointing at the tray: "Where can I put this?" At once the possessor of the tray cheerfully removed it to make more room for the newcomer so that she could work in comfort. Altogether it was a very charming episode.

It must be remembered, too, that these were children in a poor district, and this was not by any means an isolated incident of such courtesy. Generally speaking, children in a Montessori school show a great respect for the rights and properties of the other members of their little world.

FREEDOM AND RESPECT FOR AUTHORITY

Two little girls were working together composing words with the movable alphabet on a rug on the floor. They had filled the available space on the rug except for that part of it which was occupied by the large shallow box containing the movable letters. The children were still being carried along by the full tide of their creative energy and wanted to compose more words. But now the problem arose, where to put them? The idea came to one little head
152

that they might remove the box and place it on the floor. They considered this possibility for a moment, but decided against it. With a serious expression, one of them remarked: "No, we can't do that!" For a while they stood wondering what to do. A boy came by. Leaning for a moment against a large fire screen, he watched them with a sort of detached interest. They appealed to him: "Couldn't we take the box off the rug and put it on the floor? We can't make any more words." He shook his head emphatically, thus confirming their own decision. Then he replied: "No. Leave it where it is." With that he strolled away leaving the problem still unsolved. One of the little girls took up the tray again and looked longingly at the space beneath, but replaced it once more as though admonished by an inner voice.

At last the teacher came by. At once they asked her if it would be all right for them to place the tray on the floor. She, too, confirmed their decision that it was not the correct thing to do. They looked quite relieved to get this final ruling on the problem. The whole incident seemed to me to show a great respect for a sort of moral law. For certainly the children did not act from fear of punishment. There was no punishment in that school.

RIVAL FIRMS

Tommy was not quite sure what he would do next. So he looked around the room. In one corner were two boys busy making up words on a rug on the floor. This struck Tommy as being a desirable occupation; consequently he got a rug and a box of letters. He was not, however, very advanced in the art of spelling, so he walked over to the old established firm to get a few tips. Like many other imitators, he did not properly understand the original, and thus a good many of his letters got mixed up — like this, NAM (man), NUG (gun). However, he went on cheerfully just the same. As soon as he had composed each new word, he went across the room to get more ideas from the other firm. One of the latter rather resented this plagiarizing. I heard him remark petulantly to his colleague: "It isn't fair." But he took no action about it.

Some time later, returning to this end of the room, I noticed that Tommy also had taken a partner into his firm — one more capable than himself — and the business was going along briskly and independently, "under new management."

THE ENVIRONMENT HELPS UNEXPECTEDLY

It would not be freedom to put a child into an empty room and leave him to his own choice. There would be little or nothing for him to choose. But in the prepared environment of the Montessori school the child is surrounded by a great variety of attractive occupations, all of which seem to say: "Come and use me."

I saw a small girl with a piece of chalk and a drawing board, and she was trying to write. She made a few letters and then a few numbers, but all muddled up. She soon got tired of this occupation as there was nothing very definite about it. As she was going to return the little blackboard to its place, she happened to notice all the number cards from one to ten spread out in order on an adjacent table. Here was the answer to her vague dissatisfaction — something definite to do. At once she went back to her place and began copying the numbers. First she examined one of them carefully, and then went back to her place and wrote it. Then she came back and did the same for the next number, wrote that — and so on through the whole series.

The same sort of thing is always happening. A child

may be undecided what to do next, when suddenly something in the prepared environment calls out to him and shows him the way, just as a man, undecided which course to take, suddenly sees a signpost that puts him on the right path. It is, therefore, of the utmost importance that the Montessori teacher see that the environment is always kept in apple-pie order, well supplied with the various means of stimulating this self-activity.

The social environment helps, too, for one of the ·most stimulating invitations to work is seeing what other children are doing. Thus, children who are just beginning to write will often copy the sentences which more advanced children have composed on the blackboard — just for the sake of practice.

MAN IS A SOCIAL ANIMAL

A girl, about five years of age, had spent more than an hour writing out the numbers from one to thirty-nine. First she composed them with number cards on the frame specially made for the purpose and then she copied them out. It might seem to some, ignorant of the ways of children in a Montessori school, that a child could hardly take a whole hour to write thirty-nine numbers. But it must be remembered that children set themselves a remarkably high standard. Quite commonly you may see a child write a number, or a letter, five or six times, rubbing it out again and again until he thinks it is sufficiently near the ideal. When this particular child had reached the number thirty-nine, her little blackboard was full and she leaned back and regarded it with great satisfaction.

But that was not enough. Man is a social animal, and she felt the need of showing it to someone. So she stood up with the little blackboard in her hand, about to go and show it to the directress. Just at that moment she happened to catch my eye, and saw that I was watching her. At once, though I was a complete stranger, she held up her slate for me to see. I smiled and nodded approvingly. Whereupon she turned it around and showed me the other side. Again I smiled and nodded. With this she seemed quite satisfied, as if some inner need had been met. She sat down again, rubbed out all the figures, and began quietly copying out the next series from forty onwards.

Experiences of this sort are quite common with visitors to a Montessori school. Such actions on the part of the children are not to be confused with "showing off," for they are done quite naturally and without any self-consciousness. The motive behind it is far more fundamental than "showing off"; it is more like the necessity which an artist feels to show his work to a friend, or the scientist to publish the results of his research.

MUTUAL HELP

I noticed three children, aged about five, sitting at the same table and making extraordinary faces at each other. They were curving back their lips, and showing their teeth, and producing queer noises with tongue and throat. Soon they were joined by another who began making the same grimace, producing the same sounds. They put me in mind of monkeys showing their teeth! I soon discovered, however, that this was a very human and intelligent performance. To my astonishment I realized that it was no game at all but a serious business. One of the children had a sandpaper "L" before her on the table, and her little friend beside her was giving her a lesson on how to pronounce the letter exactly. She even opened her mouth and showed her small pupil how her tongue should be curled against the roof of her mouth. One of the neighbors — aged five and a half — becoming interested in the affair, corroborated this information and illustrated it by doing it himself. So thus in a few minutes another small child was fully initiated into the mystery of how properly to pronounce the letter "L"; and all this quite independently of the directress.

Dr. Montessori is always reiterating to her students that they should give children *most precise and exact instruction* as to how things are to be done. The importance of the maxim is revealed in this incident, which illustrates how, in a Montessori class, knowledge takes wings and flies from child to child.

This is one of the reasons why, other things being equal, a teacher will get better results with a class of thirty children than with ten — a very important and practical point — and one in which the Montessori system has a great advantage over the Froebel kindergarten.

THE MYSTERIOUS COMMAND

I noticed a student, about four and a half, seriously studying a slip of paper with some words on it. It was one of a little pile of half a dozen such. She was obviously not far advanced in the art of reading, and found great difficulty in making out the meaning of the sentence. At the next table was a little boy, Peter, who had been absorbed nearly all morning with some animal cards. The name of each animal was beneath the picture and he was copying them. After puzzling vainly over her sentence, the girl finally took it over to Peter. The latter quite obviously did not welcome this interruption of his work. In fact he took a reading slip from her hand in a rather brusque manner, with just such an air of annoyance as that of a manager who resented the intrusion of a visitor on a busy morning in the office. He did, however, read the phrase which was: "Run to the window." At this she thanked him, trotted to the right place, and then went back to her table and took up the next card. This one, "Go and fill a glass with water," she was able to do by herself. Some of the others she failed to decipher, and was obliged again to have recourse to her friend.

The latter clearly performed his part in the affair as a duty, and would much have preferred to get on with his own work uninterrupted. In acting thus, however, he was learning something even more important than the names of animals. It is only through a life which includes such free intercourse with others that the social virtues can develop — as all good habits develop — through activity.

In the same school, I noticed a similar incident. A small child was doing the first reading exercise, which is as follows: There is a tray full of little objects and a corresponding packet of little cards. On each of the latter is written the name of one of the objects in the tray. The exercise consists in taking a card and reading it and then placing it under the corresponding object. The scholar got stuck over the very first word, which was "Hat." She tried again and again to decipher it, making a curious hissing sound as she did so. (It would seem that "S" was her favorite letter!) At last she rose and took the card to a comrade at an adjoining table. The latter was not an expert reader herself. She gazed at the word on the card, repeating the separate letters, one after the other with great attention, "H—A—T." Then suddenly the synthesis came to her mind and she said: "Hat." The little visitor, who had been following this proceeding with marked attention, thanked her, took up the slip, and went away still looking at it and repeating to herself as she went: "H — a — t makes hat." On coming to her place, she looked for the little hat in the tray and put the card under it. Then she took up the next card, and quickly got stuck over that. Again she brought it to her friend to be helped out. And so with all the ten cards — making ten separate journeys. The other child took it all in remarkably good part and told her what each card said, answering, I noticed, a little snappishly toward the end. But, the fact remains, she did help her each of the ten times she was interrupted.

I do not recollect in all my experience as an observer or teacher ever having seen a child refuse to help another, though sometimes I have seen them fail in the attempt to do so. In such cases the inquirer generally succeeds in getting the help he is looking for from another child or from the directress.

THE DICTATION LESSON

In the examples just described, the children who helped others were passive in their attitude. They did not go out of their way to give help until they were asked to, because, quite properly, they were engaged in their own work. Sometimes, however, the desire to help arises quite spontaneously, and is so strong that it deliberately seeks expression — as in the following incident which I witnessed in a Montessori school in Berlin. There were more than thirty children in the class, only one teacher and no assistant.

In one angle of the room, Erna was writing at a table, copying a poem. On a chair quite near her, a smaller and younger girl, Gretel, was looking at the pictures in a Reading Book. Erna would be about seven and Gretel about five, and much less advanced than the former. Erna was a motherly soul with a quiet, assured manner.

As she was writing, and without looking around, Erna said to her little companion: "Read something aloud from your book."

"But I can hardly read at all," was the reply.

"No matter," said Erna encouragingly. "Try. I'll help you."

So Gretel began, very slowly and hesitantly, spelling out the words. "I a - m, am, v - e - r - y, very . . . ." Then came a long pause.

"Go on," said Erna encouragingly.

"C - o - l - d, cold?" went on Gretel with a note of interrogation, as though not sure of the word.

Erna stopped, turned around, ran her finger along the line until she came to the word. "Right!" she said and then added cheerfully, "Go on."

Gretel struggled on for another line or two and then there was another long pause. Again Erna stopped her work, looked in the book and helped her little pupil out of the difficulty.

And so it went on for about fifteen minutes, Gretel sticking at almost every line, and Erna, with surprising patience, stopping her writing to help her. At this juncture a boy came from the other end of the room and began talking to Erna about some arithmetic apparatus that he was looking for. As soon as he had gone Erna returned to her copying and, without looking up, said in a most businesslike way, "Go on."

Whereupon Gretel's little voice piped up once more and the reading continued for several more minutes. While this was going on, I noticed Erna feeling her lips with her fingers, and when the next pause came in the reading, she asked: "Gretel, have I got a mark on my lips?" Gretel examined her mouth very carefully. "No," she replied, "I don't see anything." This problem being satisfactorily settled, Erna returned to her writing, and remarked as before, "Go on."

What struck me about the whole scene was the extraordinarily natural way it all happened. The children had no idea that I, or anyone else, was listening. In fact, although I was standing near enough to hear what was going on, I had my back turned most of the time, and was pretending to be buried in a book which I had taken from an adjoining bookshelf. I am certain that the children were as unconscious of my existence as if I had been in Timbuktu.

Suddenly a bright idea occurred to Erna. "Would you like to do some writing?" she inquired.

"But I'm such a bad writer, even worse than reading," replied the modest Gretel.

"No matter!" answered the undaunted Erna. "I'll help you."

So little Gretel got down from her chair and went to find paper and pencil. (It is included in the meaning of the term prepared environment that such things be always ready and easily accessible for the children's spontaneous undertakings.)

While Gretel was seeking the materials, I went over to another part of the room to make notes on the progress of some other children whom I had also singled out for observation.

When I returned the scene had changed. Little Gretel was sitting at the table and "the little mother" (for so she seemed to me) was seated on a chair nearby, and, to my surprise, a dictation lesson was in full swing. It had been going on for some minutes, I gathered, for as I came up I heard Erna say: "When you have finished what I have given you, you must say 'Go on.'"

"Go on," piped the tiny voice obediently.

"They were sitting on a little fir tree," went on the "teacher's" voice. Erna was brooding over her small charge like a Providence, watching every word as it came slowly, very slowly, into existence. It appeared there had been a mistake in the very first word of this new sentence. And so Erna took an eraser, rubbed it out and corrected it. "Sitting . . . ," she repeated. "That's a fresh word!" she added, hurriedly, seeing Gretel about to join it to the previous one.

Another difficulty now arose. In German the double "S" is written in a special manner and Gretel did not know this. So once more there was a rubbing out and an explanation. "Oh, that's awfully hard!" exclaimed Gretel. But there was no thought of giving up. The piece chosen by Erna was obviously too difficult for the smaller child, but it never occurred to the teacher to seek out a more elementary book. However, her patience was so inexhaustible that I think she would have helped her little friend through *Webster's Dictionary.*

After a few moments there was another interruption from the same boy, who had come this time to discuss something about the eleven times table.

"Go on," came the little voice from the table, as soon as he had departed.

" . . . and . . . ," read out the teacher, and at once the little hand went to work again.

" . . . his wife . . . " (a pause).

"Go on."

" . . . walked . . . "

I felt sure *that* would stump her. It did. So the teacher wrote it down for her and then proceeded.

There was a pause while Gretel wrote this word.

" . . . on . . . "

"Oh!" exclaimed Erna in a burst of delight. "You've written that word better than I could have written it myself." No coach who had succeeded in getting his pupil through his examination could ever be more delighted than was Erna with her pupil's success. She took the exercise book in her hand and examined the word carefully, with her head a little on one side, as though it was one of the seven wonders of the world. I was so interested in this new development that I sidled a step nearer to see if I could see this masterpiece myself. At that moment Erna's eye caught mine for the first time. "Some of the letters she makes," she said, addressing me as though we had been friends all our lives, "some of her letters are even better than I could do. Look at that!" I made what seemed to me an appropriate remark, and retired as quickly as I could to the background so as to let this little drama continue its natural course without any adult intervention.

" . . . fir tree." The next word I heard through the tail of my ear, for I was pretending to be back at my book again. "Capital letter!" exclaimed Erna quickly in a warning voice. (All nouns in German are spelled with an initial capital letter.)

After a few minutes another boy, who was going to the cupboard to put his work away, passed quite near my little friends. "Look," said Erna, pulling him toward their table and pointing to Gretel's paper, "Gretel did that word (it was the famous 'on') all by herself. It's better than I could have done it!"

There was not the slightest trace of jealousy in her tone; it was pure joy at the achievement of her little friend.

How long this amazing lesson would have gone on I could not say, but, unfortunately, after another five minutes it had to stop as it was time to put all work away in preparation for lunch.

Scores of similar incidents happen every day in the various Montessori schools, but most of them pass unrecorded. They are not recorded, partly because, as happened in this case, they are not even noticed by the teacher. The other reason is that, even when they are noticed, the teacher is generally too busy to make notes.

THE GRAMMAR LESSON

I once observed a very similar incident in a Montessori school in Rome. In this case it was a boy of seven who was giving a grammar lesson to another of about the same age. It may seem surprising to some readers that any boys at that age would take an interest — and it must be remembered that it is a spontaneous interest — in so dry a subject. The Montessori grammar, however, is far from dry. It is active and dynamic with plenty of movement thrown in. Without going into details, we might just point out that the "grammar commands," which this boy was using direct the attention of the children upon objects in their environment. For instance, if it is a question of prepositions, it will draw attention to the actual relationship between various objects in the classroom. Or if — as in this particular case — it is a question of studying adjectives, the grammar commands focus the child's mind upon the qualities of certain objects in the room. Thus he may get a card with the phrase "the thick prism" written on it. Whereupon he goes and gets the thick prism and puts it next to the slip. Then, leaving the rest of the phrase as it is, he substitutes a card with the word "thin." Whereupon he goes and gets the thin prism. In this way it is visibly and dramatically brought home to him that an adjective is a word which limits a noun. Similarly with the other adjective commands. They all involve getting some particular object which visibly reveals the function of the adjective in question.

In this case, the little Italian boy had already worked through these identical exercises on a previous day, but now he was about to initiate his little friend into the same mysteries. The interesting and amusing thing about it was that, before he began, he went around the room in a most businesslike way, collecting (from memory) the various objects which he would have to use in the exercise — just as a science lecturer prepares all the apparatus necessary for his experiment before his lecture starts.

Having arranged this miscellaneous collection of objects on a table nearby, the boy sat down with his pupil and solemnly instructed him on how the thing was done. Instead, however, of having to make a number of journeys about the room as the work proceeded — e.g., to that cupboard for the red color tablet, to this for a long rod, to another for a small cube, and so on — he simply had to turn to the next table where the small teacher's foresight had made everything ready.

THE READING GAME

The directress in one of the English schools gave out little cards, each with a word written on it, one card to each of a number of children. They were sitting expectantly in a little circle. It must not be imagined that there are *no* group lessons in the Montessori system; collective lessons are used occasionally when they would be more helpful. Each child was asked to read his card to himself; then turn it over and fold his arms. The teacher asked each one in turn to come up and give her card to her and then *act* it. The cards were all verbs, written on red slips and included such words as "sleep," "dance," "draw," "weep," "walk," "sing," "run," and "jump." When a child had acted his card, the others had to guess what was written on it.

I noticed a girl who was only just beginning to read — I knew this for I had seen her unsuccessful efforts to do so in another exercise the same morning — also came along with the others, determined to join in the fun. She begged for a card and was given one. She tried desperately to make it out, but did not succeed. Before her turn came to act her word, however, she managed to attract the attention of another girl who was passing by, and whispered: "Lily, what is my word?" Lily read it and whispered: "Dance." At last it was Joyce's turn to go out into the middle. She gave up her card, turned around and made two half-hearted jumps, and then suddenly collapsed with stage fright, and asked if she could have someone join her. So she went and found her friend (the same one who had told her the word) and the two did a little dance together.

Some of the very tiny ones, who could not read at all, came and stood by, watching the proceedings with open-mouthed wonder. It seemed to them indeed a very strange and mystifying performance. They realized, however, that it had something to do with the little red slips of paper, and that learning to read was the gate of initiation into these ceremonies; and therefore it sharpened their desire to know more about the subject. (Not many children would have thought of slipping in by a side door, as Joyce had managed to do — the young gatecrasher!)

Though this was a reading lesson, it is interesting to note that it was also a grammar lesson, or at any rate the first foreshadowing of grammar. The children notice that all the words on the little red slips make you *do* something; whereas they are followed by another set of little black cards with nouns on them, and these you *can put on the objects referred to* — desk, pen, book, etc. — a thing not possible to do with the red or "doing" cards. So already, through this experience — long before any definitions are given — the children gain an intuition of the difference between words that denote *names* and words that mean *actions*.

THE MYSTERY CARDS

Often the children do this exercise without the teacher. I saw two five-year-olds, Annie and Barbara, working together on a packet of verb cards. As usually happens in these spontaneously formed groups, one of the two was the leading partner. It was Annie in this instance. The little heads bent over the cards together in a strained silence. "It — says — Button," whispered Annie at last, almost as though "it" were a person. "I'll go and get the duster while you do up the buttons on the button frame."

The next card said "Brush," so away went Annie to find a brush. Thereupon there was a great brushing of clothes, during which I noticed, with interest, that Barbara was given a lesson in how to brush clothes properly.

And so they went through the whole series: Lace, Sweep, Clean, Tie, Hook, etc. How wonderful were these insignificant looking cards to them! Each was like a magic talisman, summoning some unexpected event into existence.

ANOTHER LITTLE TEACHER

I saw a little fuzzy-haired girl putting a rug on the floor. "What's that for?" asked a visitor. "For the numbers — the tens," she replied. When the rug was duly spread out, I saw her go and get a box full of tens. Each ten consists of a little bar of ten yellow beads fastened together on a single wire. Along with the tens she brought a set of cards. On the first was written 10, on the next 20, the next 30, and so on up to 100. The exercise consists in putting down the cards and placing the corresponding number of tens next to each card — e.g., one ten next to the 10 card, two tens next to the 20 card, and so on. This little girl, however, did not properly understand the principle involved. She placed the first card, the 10, on the rug and then, instead of putting *one* ten-bead-bar next to it, she counted out *ten*, that is ten-bead-bars, or one hundred. She clearly regarded each ten-bead-bar as a unit instead of a ten. I was longing to help her and put her right, but as a visitor I might not interfere. After a few moments, however, a little boy passing by observed what she was doing. At once he stopped and explained her mistake to her. Then he started her off on the right track by doing a few examples for her. After this she carried on the exercise correctly right up to the end. In this case I don't think the boy was actually moved by any particularly altruistic motives. He simply could not bear to see the thing done wrongly; it offended his sense of the fitness of things — like a picture hanging crooked.

Which reminds me of another amusing incident. A lad of about five was working with the sensorial geometry apparatus. The particular exercise consisted in spreading out on a rug various cards representing different geometrical figures — squares, circles, triangles, polygons, etc. This done, the next thing is to take the corresponding wooden insets from the drawers of the geometric cabinet and place each on the appropriate card. He had been working in this way for a long time and had filled the entire rug with figures. One of the cards must have been missing from the series, for when he came to the end he found that he had one wooden inset left over for which there was no corresponding card. The little fellow found himself in a quandary. There were all the other cards, each mated with its corresponding wooden inset, but this last inset was an annoying anomaly. There was no place for it in the scheme of things. It was a blot on an otherwise pleasant landscape, a jarring note in the general harmony. What to do with it? For some minutes he considered the problem with a worried expression. Once more his hand, holding the wooden inset, hovered over all the other cards, trying to find a place for it only to discover once more that all the cards were already occupied. Then suddenly he had a brainwave and he slid the offending polygon out of sight under the edge of the rug. It was the best solution he could think of, based obviously on the principle "out of sight, out of mind." After this he went and sat on a chair nearby for some minutes serenely surveying the results of his work with great satisfaction.

A GREAT DISCOVERY

One day when I was observing in a Montessori class at a convent school in London, I saw a little girl, aged about six, looking with an absorbed interest at a slip of paper on her table, on which she had been writing some figures.

Actually she had been working out for herself, with the help of the multiplication board and beads, the nine times table. In the Montessori system the children work out all their tables in this way. It is a form of individual research. I was sitting quite near the child and could see that she had got down as far as $9 \times 8 = 72$. But she did not carry on the work by putting out the next row of nine beads to make $9 \times 9 = 81$.

Instead she took up the paper on which she had recorded her previous researches up to date, and with the paper in her hand went to show it to her friend Jenny, who was sitting two or three yards away at another table. "Look, Jenny," she said, pointing down to the paper with her forefinger, "isn't it funny? It goes 1, 2, 3, 4, 5, 6, 7 in this column (the tens) and 9, 8, 7, 6, 5, 4, 3, 2, on the other column" (the units).

This was the staggering and unexpected discovery which she had made, and her whole being was full of the wonder of it. Jenny was immersed in a grammar exercise on singulars and plurals and was in no mood to appreciate such a mathematical marvel. In fact she was about as much interested as Sir Isaac Newton's housekeeper might have been if that great scientist had tried to explain to her his newly discovered law of gravity at the very moment she was absorbed in making strawberry jam.

Jenny just looked at the paper indifferently and acknowledged the information with a polite nod and a smile, upon which she returned to her singulars and plurals.

My poor little scientist was obviously disappointed. She had made an epoch-making discovery and no one in the room seemed in the least interested. All the other children were bent over their work and, as it happened, even the directress was not in sight.

At that moment, her eyes happened to meet mine. I was apparently just sitting there doing nothing and so she felt that she would not be disturbing me. At any rate it was worth trying. So, her excitement and overpowering desire to communicate her discovery overcame her shyness, and she came up to me with her precious paper. Pointing as before, she said: "Isn't it funny? It goes 9, 8, 7, 6 . . . etc." just as she had said to Jenny.

To tell the truth, I myself had never noticed this sequence before, and I wonder whether the reader has.

At least I was able to enter into the wonder of her discovery with genuine enthusiasm.

This was all she wanted. A need had been satisfied and she went quietly back to her place to continue her work.

On another occasion I saw a much smaller child become very excited after she had been working with the color tablets. She turned to her neighbor and exclaimed enthusiastically: "Your lips are red! Your lips are red!"

THE STOLEN CHAIR

A group of very small boys was having what appeared to be an arithmetical conference in the middle of the room, the subject of their discussion being the ten number rods. Three of them had brought chairs, and were sitting there, looking on with astonishing gravity at the boy with the rods. The fourth member of their committee had no chair and so he went to find one. He selected one which happened to be placed beside a table at which a little girl was working. She seemed to regard this vacant chair as her property, although she was actually sitting on another. However, he insisted on taking it away. The little girl resented this high-handed proceeding so strongly that for some time she held up her hand, trying to attract the teacher's attention. Nothing happened, however, and so, making the best of it, she went and got another button frame and set to work at it. A short time afterwards, the arithmetical conference having broken up, I saw the same little boy bring back the chair, quite spontaneously, and place it by the same table. At this the little girl's face brightened, and she smiled and nodded her thanks.

THE DIDACTIC MATERIAL SECURES ATTENTION

Under the old system of collective class teaching, a considerable portion of the teacher's time and energy was expended in trying to hold the attention of the children to the subject in hand. If their attention wandered, as it frequently did, she had to bring it back again by various devices, much as a sheep dog is kept busy holding together a flock of sheep. Under the Montessori system the attention of the children to their work is secured by means of the various teaching materials and the activities to which they give rise.

The great psychologist, Professor William James, spoke of "that extreme mobility of the attention with which we are familiar in children . . . which makes their first lessons such rough affairs . . . . The faculty of voluntarily bringing back a wandering attention, over and over again, is at the very root of judgment, character and will . . . . An education which should improve this faculty would be education *par excellence.*" One of the most striking revelations of the Montessori method was just this, that it showed that small children, even at three years of age, can and do display an astonishing degree of voluntary attention. This attention is not artificially stimulated and sustained by the teacher, but is fixed spontaneously on an object and corresponds to an internal impulse.

I noticed a little girl who seemed to be very much interested in the little rubber band which bound together the reading slips which she had just taken from the cupboard. She played with it, stretched it out, wrapped it around her finger, flipped it so as to make a musical note, and so on. But it presented no *lasting* interest to her. After a while, she put it down and her attention reverted quite naturally to the reading slips which were lying on her table, awaiting only her attention to speak their mysterious commands.

In the same school I noticed another tot, coming from the cupboard, carrying a piece of cardboard on which was a packet of number cards. She was holding the cardboard not quite horizontally and so the packet of cards began to slide toward the edge, but she managed to tilt it up again just before the cards fell off. But then the packet began to slip down toward the other side of the cardboard. So now she began amusing herself by tilting the board backwards and forwards, stopping, with considerable skill, just in time to prevent the cards falling off.

If the teacher had noticed this, she would probably have indicated that it was not the right use to make of the number cards, but, as there were more than forty children in the room, the busy teacher had not noticed it at all. This little game amused the child for some five or ten minutes and then died a natural death. Thereupon she settled down to the serious work for which the cards were intended.

INTELLECTUAL HUNGER

I saw Jane get a reading exercise from the cupboard. It consisted of pictures and corresponding cards with names, one name to each card. It happened to be Set 5 and the words in it, such as "Nurse" and "Horse," were too hard for her. She was obliged, therefore, to give it up. She went back quickly, procured Set 2 instead, and immediately spread out the pictures on her table. She was desperately anxious to do the exercise. Every action was precipitate. She reminded me of a dog who knows that his food is being prepared and runs up and down whining in his agitation. She was fairly rushing at this intellectual food. But even in Set 2 most of the words seemed beyond her. At last she made out one, M - A - N, MAN. How delighted she was! With what joy did she place the card triumphantly under the picture of the man! She even stroked him caressingly, as though he had become her friend.

CAUGHT BY THE SILENCE

Without saying a word, the directress placed a card with the word "SILENCE" printed on it in a conspicuous place. At once a number of children stopped working and put down their hands on their laps. Some whispered softly to others near them, and they, too, at once stopped working. After three or four minutes, without a word being said by the directress, all the children in the room had stopped working and were sitting motionless. All except one who was facing away from the notice. She was still absorbed in her occupation and was singing gently to herself as she worked — to the mild amusement of the rest who were patiently waiting for the silence game to begin.

LEARNING THE ALPHABET

Eileen was a quaint little mite about four and a half years old. She was sitting in a corner and the directress was giving her a lesson on the letter "F." And then, very slowly and solemnly, she traced the sandpaper contour of the letter with her first and second fingers, saying "ff" "ff" as she did so, in short explosions like a diminutive locomotive. As she came to the end of the letter she released her hand from the card with a dainty staccato movement which seemed to correspond with a sudden suspension of concentration.

The directress now went away and left her to it. Eight or nine times she repeated this process and then carefully put the letter "F" down on a corner of her table. She now took up the next letter in the pile, which happened to be "E." Rising from her place, she solemnly went off with it in her hand to find the directress, who, as it happened, was now busy attending to someone else. Eileen did not "butt in" but waited patiently until the directress was at liberty to attend to her. (This discipline of having to control her immediate impulse, in order to respect the rights of others, is as important a part of her training as the actual learning of the letters.) After a few moments, the directress saw her, took the letter and showed her how to feel around it, at the same time pronouncing the sound it represented. Thereupon Eileen returned to her table almost embracing the letter as she went — and then settled down to feel and pronounce it again and again. The letter "E" being finished with for the time being, Eileen then selected another letter, and with it went off once more in search of the directress. After being duly initiated into this, she returned to her table to practice it many times. And so it went on for at least another half-dozen letters, since Eileen seemed insatiable in her desire to learn them. At last she had to stop as it was time to pack up and go home.

LOVE OF ORDER

While Eileen was away on her first trip (with the letter "E"), a little boy happened to pass her table. On it he noticed the pile of letters, but one letter (the "F") was not in the pile, but left lying at the corner of the table. Without even stopping, he picked up the letter as he went by and returned it to the pile from which it had come. The curious thing about this action was that it seemed almost unconscious. The boy had obviously no intention of staying at the table, nor of using the cards himself, but in passing he had become aware of something in the environment which was not in its right place. And so, in response to an inner need, he had almost automatically put it right.

A MONTESSORI EXAMINATION

About a week after this episode, I visited the same class. I saw Eileen, who was still wrapped up in her zeal for the sandpaper letters. This time she had spread more than a dozen letters out on her table. She had an air of calm expectancy. Soon the directress arrived and sat down beside her. She had come to test Eileen's knowledge of the letters and their sounds. It was not a competitive examination and there was no external reward. Eileen was truly excited — yet it was not the excitement of showing off but simply the joy of testing her new powers.

"Show me the one that says 'ff'," said the teacher, and Eileen solemnly picked up the "F" card. "And now the one that says 'ah'," and so on through all the others. Eileen would have easily got 90% on that examination.

Then the directress put two of the letters together and explained the principle of running the two sounds together to make a word. I was pleased to see that she had an additional interest in the letters and now could, if she liked, compose certain words with the movable type.

Before she went away the directress taught her another letter, "L". This seemed to Eileen an especially attractive one, because she ran her fingers over it twenty times without stopping, saying aloud "le, le, le." At this juncture she paused for a while and had a conversation with a passing boy. When he had gone off, she started again and did the same letter another ten times. Then she rested for a while, after which she did it another five times. Altogether she must have made the movement of that letter with her fingers and said its sound at least forty times. She went on voluntarily studying the letters of the alphabet for well over an hour and a quarter.

SPONTANEOUS BALANCING EXERCISE

Margaret was waiting to speak to the directress, who was teaching a small group. I was amused to see how she put in the time, walking up and down the line very carefully, one foot just in front of the other, just as they do during the special time devoted to these exercises (though, of course, she had to do it without music this time). The same day I noticed another child, a little boy

176

on the way to the cupboards, doing something similar, only he was walking carefully along an *imaginary* line.

BUILDING THE BAGDAD RAILWAY

The thousand bead chain is a wonderful and exciting affair, veritably an experience to be lived through.

To begin with, there is the sheer length of it. It is so enormously long and unwieldy that you cannot manage it alone, without risk of being entangled in its coils like those of a boa constrictor. Actually it stretches from one end of their little Montessori world to the other — sometimes even extending several yards beyond it into the passage. For it is more than thirty feet long!

Generally two or three children unite to work at it in a self-constituted company. The first thing to do is to stretch out the monster's huge length, in a straight line if possible, along the floor. This is an undertaking comparable to laying the Bagdad railway across the Persian desert. The small company meets to discuss the best route. Having decided on a home base, they begin laying it down. Before long they find themselves passing through strange territories, across uncharted regions. Very often it is necessary to negotiate with the inhabitants of these regions for a right of way, between two tables it may be, or to beg a passage by asking someone to move his rug. Sometimes these established tribes are rather hostile and inclined to resent all intrusion into their established domains. But, in time, differences are adjusted and the great work goes forward. The gang usually works under the leadership of one individual who has a deeper knowledge of what is to be done, and he directs the operation.

And what an operation it is! Will they never come to the end of it? Such walking up and down, such pulling and straightening, such stepping backward and forward, over and along it! Sometimes sentinels must be stationed at special places where there is a lot of traffic, to warn passers-by not to tread on the chain.

My simile of a railway line, I see, has occurred to one of the little boys engaged, for, slipping away from the foreman, he has taken a hundred bead chain with ten cars (each a ten bead bar) and is dragging it along the line in imitation of a train and making a puffing noise as he goes.

At last it is all laid out. Now the chief engineer is coming along to direct the next stage in the proceeding. It consists in what appears to be the laying out of the various stations along the line. These are the hundred number cards. Upon each is printed, in large red figures, the various hundreds up to a thousand — 100, 200, 300, 400 and so on. Each card must be placed at its proper position along the line, until at last they come to the big 1,000 card which is the terminus.

Several very tiny children, who are still at the stage of the purely sensorial materials, are looking on with great interest, almost with awe. Some day they, too, will arrive at the stage of grappling with this wonderful numerical monster with all its golden coils, just as, some day, they know it will also fall to their lot to write sentences on the blackboard as the older children are doing.

But what is happening now? Look at that little fellow over there at the far end of the chain. Gracious! He has embarked on the colossal enterprise of counting each one of those separate thousand beads from end to end, touching each particular bead with his fingers as he goes along. What a journey lies before him! Again I am reminded of the simile of the desert, but this time of the long monotonous journey of a caravan. What mysterious instinct urges this little traveler on? What hope of attainment?

We are so apt to think of the study of numbers simply as means to an end that we forget that for the child it can, and should, be an end in itself.

Sometimes indeed the journey is so long, along this golden road of the thousand bead chain, that the little pilgrims are overcome with fatigue before they reach the end. Sometimes a child will come up to the directress and say: "Please, I've counted to 537 and I'm tired. May I put a mark down on the chain and go on with it again tomorrow? And this is done. Next morning, refreshed with a night's rest, the little traveler continues his journey to the end, i.e., to one thousand. What makes the children spontaneously undertake these and similar prodigious exercises, involving such long and patient labor? No teacher would ever think of *imposing* such Herculean tasks on any child. The explanation is an interesting and revealing one.

In ordinary methods, when the teacher is quite sure that the child has really mastered a fact, or group of facts, he thinks: "Good! Now he is ready for the next step." But, in point of fact, that is not the way the mind of a free child works when he is at liberty to choose his own occupations.

A child chooses to work with a certain piece of apparatus just because he knows it and loves it. Montessori was never tired of saying that these "immense and patient labors are a form of love."

The child who is counting along the thousand bead chain knows exactly what he is doing. He has already become acquainted with the anatomy of numbers. He is aware of the position of each number with which he is dealing in the hierarchy of numbers. Children are often taught in ordinary schools to speak of, and calculate with, the symbols for hundreds and thousands without ever having gained any clear notion of what they really signify. Consequently they speak of them with as little real understanding as we do when we talk of billions and trillions.

I remember reading an article in the *Daily Mail* by a former Indian treasury official. It was entitled "On Counting Millions." "Few persons," said the writer, "can have any clear idea of what is meant by a million rupees unless they have seen and handled the sum in actual cash . . . . Ten million pounds in gold weighs about ninety tons; in silver Indian rupees, more than seventeen hundred tons — a small ship load." The writer then went on to describe his experience in counting the vast wealth stored in the reserve treasury of the government of India. He concluded with these words: "By the end of the day, one begins to realize what a million of money really means."

Similarly, a child who has worked with the thousand bead chain — spread it to its full length on the floor, counted it from one end to the other — knows what a thousand really means. After this experience, it will never happen to him to confuse hundreds with the thousands as children so often do. He has too much respect for the thousand!

CHAPTER FIVE
A VISIT TO LILLIPUT

CHILDREN, AS EVERY PARENT KNOWS, ARE INCESSANTLY ACTIVE. This is because they are growing; for growth and activity always go together, a fact which many parents overlook.

In the good home and the good nursery school, therefore, provision must be made for children to be constantly active. But here we come up against a point of cardinal importance. *What kind of activity?* This is the crux of the whole matter, for not any kind of activity will do. There is no magical educational value in activity as such. This is a point misunderstood by many of our educational authorities, as anyone can see for himself if he visits some of our so-called progressive schools where children are allowed to "do what they like," and, in so doing, learn little besides aggressiveness and bad manners.

But the child is not a cat or a lizard. He is not a little animal at all; nor is he, as many of our modern psychologists affirm, "just a bundle of instincts." He is infinitely higher than all this, he is the "son of man." And as such he comes into this world possessing not only a tiny undeveloped body but also an immortal soul endowed with the sovereign powers of intelligence and will.

The essential drama of the child's life, from birth to his fourth or fifth year, is bound up with the tremendous problem of establishing a right relationship between these two diverse elements — soul and body, mind and matter, will and muscle. Hence the desirable activities, which are going to assist the child to develop in the way God intended him to, are those which help him to weld together these contrasting elements in his nature into an ever more unified and harmonious personality.

All this may sound rather theoretical. So let us descend at once into the sphere of the practical for, as the saying is, "an ounce of practice is worth a pound of theory." Therefore, I would advise anyone who wishes to verify the truth of these statements to visit a good Montessori school.

In one of these I spent an enchanting hour in the babies' room. In fact I was so fascinated by what I saw there, that, even though my time was limited, I could not tear myself away to see what was going on in the class above. By the "babies," I mean the under fives, of whom there were forty in the one room in the charge of two Montessori directresses.

It is impossible to describe what all these forty children were doing. It would take a whole book, and so a few examples taken at random must suffice. Just as I entered the room I almost tripped over a child of three and a half who, with paints and brush and a piece of paper almost as big as himself spread out on the floor, was working at a design which Picasso might have envied. A yard away, at one of the little tables, an equally small girl was busy taking a diminishing series of wooden cylinders out of ten corresponding sockets from a block of wood and then trying to fit each back again into its right socket.

THE RICE POURER
My attention was next caught by a young fellow of two and a half who was carrying a small round tray across the room like a waiter. I moved nearer and discovered a small jug and two glasses on it. The jug contained grains of uncooked rice. It was a difficult job for this miniature waiter to hold the tray horizontally and walk along at the same time, in and out among the tables and the other children on the floor. Eventually he arrived safely at an empty table, whereupon, with an air of great satisfaction, he

placed the tray upon it and sat down himself in front of it. Then, with that same look of intense seriousness which I had observed on the face of the child with the cylinders, he began very carefully to pour the dry grains of rice into the two small glasses. When he had done this he poured the rice back again from the glasses into the jug, and did the whole process over again many times. In spite of his efforts, after he had been working for a quarter of an hour, a good many grains of rice had fallen on the floor under his table and chair.

THE TIDINESS BRIGADE

Suddenly, out of the blue, appeared Sally, a child of four and a half, with a miniature broom, and she began to sweep the grains together. I was just wondering how she would manage to get them off the floor when, again quite unexpectedly and from nowhere in particular, a third small actor arrived to play her part in this spontaneous interlude. She could not have been more than three and a half and she brought a small dustpan and brush. At once she brushed the grains of rice into her dustpan and marched off to the other end of the room, where she threw the sweepings into a waste basket.

All those taking part in this small drama did so quite independently of the teacher. In fact the teacher did not even know that it was going on, for she was kneeling on the floor at the far end of the room with her back toward us, helping two small boys who were doing something on a mat. This freedom to act for and by themselves gives the children unceasing opportunities to take part in a real social life, in which they can, and do, help each other. All over the room it was the same. The children were going about their own jobs independently of the teacher, going to her only when they got stuck, or to show her what they had done, or to ask her to show them something fresh to do.

INDIRECT PREPARATIONS FOR WRITING

At least a dozen of the children who were sitting at the tables were occupied in shading in designs with colored pencils. These designs they had made themselves with the help of a series of geometric forms — circles, rectangles, triangles — cut out of metal. The children put down these metal insets on their paper and then trace them, very often combining two or three shapes to make a more interesting and complicated pattern. They love doing this by the hour and the directress lets them continue as long as they like.

I decided to go to the other end of the room to see what was happening on the mat where the teacher was instructing the two small boys. She was dictating words, which they composed on the mat with large movable letters. The boys were taking the letters out of a tray-like box with twenty-six divisions, like a large compositor's type box. Already the words "hand," "time" and "sofa" had come into existence and the boys were eager for the teacher to suggest new words. This, too, was not actually writing; but, like the colored designs, was a preparation for it. In this exercise the children were, in fact, tackling the problem of spelling by itself, in isolation, unhampered by the effort of writing the letters — on the Montessori principle of dealing with one difficulty at a time.

At another table two children had spread out a number of large sandpaper letters, each mounted on a piece of cardboard, and were feeling over these letters with the tips of their writing fingers, at the same time saying aloud the phonetic sounds they stood for. So here we had another indirect preparation for writing. Still another came to light as Felicity (four next month) came up to show me a piece of tracing paper on which she had traced in rows the letters S, M, C, and T. The teacher told me that this was the first time she had done this exercise and I was astonished at the accuracy with which she had traced over the letters written on the card beneath. One can understand why, with all these preparatory exercises, these same children will be writing by the time they are six.

THE YOUNG JANITOR

While I was still watching the group on the mat, a small individual, with an apron on, came and stood expectantly beside the teacher, waiting with surprising patience to catch her attention. As soon as he did so, he solemnly announced: "I have finished." "Finished what?" I wondered. Then following their glances I saw a wooden bench by the side of the room with a basin of water near it, together with a small scrubbing brush and a piece of soap. The young fellow had just finished scrubbing it from one end to the other. "How nicely you have done it!" said the teacher, and off he went, pleased as Punch, to empty the dirty water into a bucket which came well up to his thighs. Then he returned without a word, untied his apron strings and hung the garment on one of the stands provided.

"What will the young fellow do next?" I wonder. No one knows except the Omniscient, for the child is quite free to decide for himself. After a few minutes' silent deliberation, a choice is made. Having apparently satisfied the practical side of his nature, aesthetic considerations now claim his attention. He procures paints, water and a large piece of paper, and proceeds to express himself with great seriousness and astonishing dexterity. (Remember, Robin is only three years of age.)

His efforts produce a somewhat rainbow effect, for he is obviously experimenting in colors and makes a series of horizontal splashes, using one color at a time. This done, he proceeds to another kind of experiment and begins mixing colors on his palette. As he does so, new ones appear and disappear, until in the end there remains a sort of universal grey.

COLOR MATCHING

At this moment a little girl, whom I had never seen before in my life, came up to me and said: "Will you please come and show me how to do my colors?" She took me by the hand and led me across the room to a mat on the floor. On this were a number of rectangular pieces of wood, all the same shape and size, but painted in different colors. Actually they were painted in pairs — two reds, two mauves, two greens, and so on. The exercise consisted in mixing them all up and then pairing them. As it happened, I knew the aim of this exercise and was able to start her off. But actually I am the last person in the world to be of very much assistance in that sphere because I happen to have a defective color sense and confuse reds and greens. Happily, however, she grasped the idea at once and I left her working much better than I could ever have done. This incident illustrates perfectly the principle that, under the Montessori system, the children learn as much, if not more, from the materials than from the teacher.

Not far away, on another mat, two more children were at work with color tablets; but theirs was a different exercise. Instead of matching colors they were grading them, that is, they had a whole group of nine blues, varying from very light to a very dark blue. This game, if you can call it so, consisted in placing all the blues against each other in shades of varying intensity, from the darkest to the lightest. And so with all the other colors. Very beautiful these sixty-three shades looked, all spread out on the mat in the bright morning sunshine, and so did the children arranging them.

I drifted over to the corner where I had left Robin experimenting with colors to see his latest production. But he had gone, disappeared somewhere into the roomful of children; and in his place was an exceedingly bright and beautiful child called Stephanie. I had noticed her earlier and had watched for a few moments as she had composed the numbers from one to ten with blue counters. She did this in a special way which brought out the difference between odd and even numbers. Apparently she felt the need to turn from science to art as had Robin after his scrubbing.

THE YOUNG GIOTTO

Stephanie was four and a half; nearly two years older than Robin and correspondingly more advanced. In fact, of all the astonishing things I saw that morning, I think what Stephanie did now was the most remarkable. She took her paintbrush in her hand and then, without any fuss or hesitation, with one sweeping movement made an almost perfect circle. I was so astounded that I felt people simply wouldn't believe me if I told them about it. And so, bending down, I said to this miniature Giotto: "Would you like to give me that painting?" Very politely, very firmly, scarcely looking up from her work, she replied in a quiet voice: "No, I want to keep it." "Well," I said, "would you like to do me another?" "No," she replied with the same quiet certainty, "I only want to do one painting this morning." So that was that!

The teacher happened to be passing by at that moment

and I mentioned this conversation to her. "I am not surprised," she said with a smile. "It's wonderful how they cherish their own paintings." I felt justly rebuked for my acquisitiveness, and could not but admire the profound respect which the teacher showed for this tiny child's personality. After all, souls have no sizes and the soul of a child is as complete, in its way, as the soul of an adult.

My self-respect was somewhat restored the next moment by the advent of Yvonne, who had come for the third time to ask me to see how she matched her colors. She, at any rate, had some respect for my artistic judgment and did not regard me as a Philistine.

A RECONCILIATION

As I wandered off in search of further adventures, I heard a crash, followed by a howl of misery. It was our young waiter. Stewart had deliberately knocked over the jug, spilling the rice on the floor.

"He's the roughest boy in the class," whispered the teacher, "he hasn't normalized yet." "But, " she continued, "he bears the children no ill will, really, and he quickly becomes reconciled to his victims and makes friends with them. Indeed I sometimes think he does these dreadful things in order to enjoy the thrill of making it up afterwards."

While the teacher had been effecting a reconciliation between the waiter and the tough guy, Sally arrived again out of nowhere, prompt as a fire engine, with her broom, and had started clearing up the mess with the same zest as before.

SOCIETY IN MINIATURE

In this brief description I have singled out a few individual children, here and there, from the crowd and described what they were doing. But you must remember that there were more than forty children in the room and each was doing something on his own. These few isolated examples, therefore, give no idea of the immense variety and wealth of occupations that were going on — still less a correct impression of the atmosphere which prevailed in that little society.

This Montessori classroom does not really strike you as being a schoolroom at all in the ordinary sense of the word. It could be more accurately described as an active society, in which both individual and collective life develop spontaneously from moment to moment. These children are in fact independent social entities. Each directs himself in a social life which is carried on in an environment of which they are collectively the masters.

They are independent because they function for themselves. Already, at two, three, four and five years of age, they are doing for themselves all manner of things which are usually done for children at those ages by adults. They dress, wash, tidy themselves and their environment, choose their own occupations, tackle their own problems, deal with emergencies as they arise — individually and collectively — without the help of any adult. What a wonderful training in self-reliance!

CANTEEN EXTRAORDINARY

Lunch time had arrived and the children went downstairs quietly to their diningroom. A long, low table, about the height of my knee, was placed along the wall, and on it, in order, plates, knives, forks, a meat dish, gravy and vegetable dishes. In front of this "help yourself" counter was the cutest queue you ever saw in your life. Every single member of it under five years and all waiting *patiently* for their turn. One by one these tiny people

189

passed along in front of the table, solemnly helped themselves to cutlery and the various dishes — taking neither too much nor too little — and then went off to sit at their places at three or four larger tables. Again I could not help thinking: "This is not a school. It is a society." This last glimpse of it seemed to sum up all that I have written with regard to their independence.

But what about the teacher? I have said very little about her. Does she not also belong to this society? Certainly she does, and in a sense she is the most important member of it. But she does not dominate the scene like an overbearing "School Marm" with strident, sergeant major voice. She is there primarily to minister to the needs of these expanding personalities. She is like the sunshine in whose genial presence the buds unfold. Her role can be best described in the words of the supreme Teacher when He said: "He that is greatest among you, let him be as one that serves."

SUPPLEMENT A

THE JOY OF LEARNING

The U. S. has all but forgotten Maria Montessori, the practical Italian idealist who founded her own brand of progressive education in 1907. Though once Americans acclaimed her, John Dewey's permissive disciples pooh-poohed her as too rigid, and only in Europe have Montessori schools made real headway. But last week, in a handsome new building in Greenwich, Conn., the nation's only "pure" Montessori school was dedicated. Whitby school is startling on at least two counts: it was founded by firmly anti-permissive Roman Catholics, and its old Montessori methods turn out to be a showcase of nearly every "new" idea that U. S. education has lately discovered.

Whitby is proudly "a work school, not a play school," and in their uniform grey skirts and shorts the children at first seem unduly solemn. Silence fills the classrooms; tears and giggles are rare; even teachers speak in near whispers. The visitor is sure that something is drastically wrong. Actually, the children are absorbed in a series of graded "jobs" that each feels compelled to complete — on his own. With almost no visible goading, Whitby's kids learn numbers at three, write at four, read at five, parse sentences at seven. Whitby is at least two years ahead of other private schools and three years ahead of public schools.

COME TO THE STABLE

Whitby is the creation of intense, redheaded Nancy McCormick Rambusch, 34, the Milwaukee-born wife of a church designer, and mother of two, who picked up her passion for Montessori methods while studying languages at the University of Paris. Trained as a Montessori teacher, she began with a small nursery group in her Manhattan apartment. Moving to Connecticut a few years later, she found fellow Catholic neighbors eager to try Montessori teaching, and in 1958 opened Whitby School in a renovated stable; naming it after the ancient Yorkshire abbey where Caedmon, the poet-stableboy, sang his verses.

Headmistress Rambusch was so successful that at last her neighbors began raising $260,000 to build a full-scale school on 37 acres. Opened in January, it now has 150 children aged three to twelve (many of them non-Catholic) and 13 teachers, including recruits from Montessori schools in France, England and Ireland. Whitby is headquarters of the newly formed American Montessori Association, and as such is training a dozen Americans to launch new Montessori schools across the U. S.

ORDER & SELF-DISCIPLINE

Whitby's inspiration, Maria Montessori, who died in 1952 at 81, was a mathematical prodigy and the first woman to get an M.D. at the University of Rome. Physician Montessori became an educator by salvaging feeble-minded children. By giving them things to touch and twist with their hands, she got their brains to function responsively. Soon the *Dottoressa* had supposedly moronic pupils outstripping normal children on public school examinations.

The soul of a child, argued Montessori, develops through "periods of sensitivity," when he has a preternatural bent to walk, talk, or advance in some other respect. These periods must be nurtured; the child must be allowed to take utmost advantage of his yearning to master chaos. Since success encourages learning, the child must also move at his own pace, step by step, gaining confidence through competence. To guarantee all this, Montessori developed what she called "the prepared environment" — a system in essence much like today's programed learning.

SEEING & STRETCHING

In 1907 she set up a school in Rome for obstreperous slum kids, using an arsenal of ingenious devices that moved from the sensory to the abstract. By handling and copying letters cut out of cardboard, the kids at four simply fell into writing and then reading. By feeling beads strung on wires in units of ten, they "saw" numbers and learned to compute in their heads. With the teacher acting only as guide, each child worked alone at his own little table or on a small rug, where he could lay out the beads and blocks, and incidentally stretch his muscles. Yet the children, divided into three-year age groups, stimulated one another as though in a family — precisely the advantage of the now much-touted ungraded primary school.

At Whitby School last week, the children, uninterrupted by any "rest" bell, worked happily, rarely disturbed one another, automatically tidied up after each task. To learn the continents, three-year-olds used special jigsaw puzzles. To strengthen muscles for early writing, they traced complex metal plates that also introduced formal geometrical shapes. To practice the alphabet, one tot used big cards with the letters pasted on in sandpaper that he could feel. Four-year-olds used cut-out letters to spell the names of animals in pictures; many wrote the names, and several five-year-olds sat quietly reading books to themselves.

By endlessly rearranging "golden beads," the children quickly learn the rational order of tens, hundreds and thousands, then addition, multiplication, subtraction and division, in that logical order, going on to square roots and the binominal theorem at the age of six. They are so fascinated with numbers that they sit around adding enormous sums for fun, or writing higher and higher numbers on long strips of paper. "I'm going to 60,000 today," said one somber four-year-old last week, as the teacher handed him another yard of paper.

Whitby's main problem is adapting Montessori self-discipline to U. S. children. "These are American kids," says Headmistress Rambusch. "They check their guns at the door, and we can't escape the fact that they need activity." From the intent look of her kids, who confine their whoops and hollers entirely to the playground, she seems to have the problem in hand. Whitby is well launched in a pursuit not always found in U. S. schools: "introducing the joy of learning to children at an early age."

SUPPLEMENT B

THE SOPHIA SCHOOL IN SANTA MONICA, CALIFORNIA

(From a talk given at Parents' Night, November 12, 1960)*

When introducing a new educational system into a community, it is normal to expect that there would be some clashes of opinion. However, though I had anticipated them, I discovered that there really wasn't much controversy between us. We all have the same concern for our children; the same anxieties, fears, and hopes. Also, in talks with some of you I have learned about your bewilderments, and, therefore, know that we all sometimes share feelings of disillusionment. But if we go a little deeper we find that even though *we* do not have too many clashes, many do exist in the world of today and they certainly do not bring us truth.

The political situation gives us perfect examples of misunderstanding, misjudgement, and man's inability to communicate. In our society today man has learned to speak, but in his haste he has nothing to say. He has learned to build a cheap radio, but the programs are even cheaper. He is hard at work at television, making the channels become stronger while the programs become weaker. A jingle fits right in the middle of a concert; or a flat, tasteless commercial interrupts a play by Shaw or Shakespeare. Banalities, bad taste, and bad manners of children have to be taken along with the rest. Commercials shout louder than a Greek drama, and it is not only in radio and television that we notice this. Elsewhere, the cover becomes more important than the book; the wrapping more important than the present; the advertisement more important than the product; and the anticipation more important than

* This and the following piece are reprinted with permission from Sophos, a Montessori Quarterly published by the Friends of Montessori, 1315 20th Street, Santa Monica, California.

the feast. We live in the age of adoration of the empty shell. Emotion and feeling have replaced thought.

The clashes of today are clashes of emotion and not of opinion, for the simple reason that the masses' thinking powers are kept under sedation of false luxury, false security, and false freedom. No wonder we parents have a task almost too heavy for our shoulders. In the midst of all this, how can we keep our children free from the spirit of materialism and bribery? . . . "Be the first one on your block to have this brand new nicky nack toy," says the commercial. "Tell your mother where she can buy it." So the child runs out: "Mamma, the man says you have to buy a nicky nack toy tonight." Always we are interrupted and bombarded by created needs and manufactured wishes and suggestions. This becomes second nature.

Now we bring our child to a Montessori school. Here the provisions are mostly spiritual. The needs revealed in the child are down-to-earth, simple, honest, and have come up from the inner spirit of the child without strong, shouting stimulants from the outside. Here the child finds patience, humility, and silence. Instead of thousands of suggestions from so-called experts, he finds freedom to improve, to help, and to even correct little mistakes. Instead of having his mind constantly overpowered by well-meaning but nevertheless dominant adults, the child finds tranquility. "Help me to do it by myself." "Help me to do the thing that is right, not the thing that is easy." I daresay, the Montessori method is a method of the mind.

Even though we start out with concrete materials, they are only the media which enlighten the mind on its way into the abstract world of thought.

Montessori reveals order and logic. Little by little the child learns to conquer himself. He makes mistakes all right, but isn't he human? The only way to ride a bike is to get on the thing and try. In Dutch we have a proverb: "Het is geen schand' te vallen, 't is schand' niet op te staan" —"it is no shame to fall, it is only a shame not to get up again."

We have had beautiful examples of both this past month, and as we have had good results in school we would like to help you along at home in the Montessori way. Therefore, at home, also, give your child quiet, order, and freedom (not lawlessness—which I will explain later). Give him quiet, not too much television, radio or Hi-Fi. Listen and enjoy silence with him. The song of a bird or the sound of the ocean or just each other's company without words. This is first preparation to meditation. Gradually, the child learns to use his own mind. The silence is the prepared environment for the development of thought.

Give him order; the framework he builds his happiness around. Set times for meals, play, bed, and last, but not least, television programs. Let the parent select suitable programs from which the child is allowed to make his own choice, then have him stick to that choice. In this manner we respect his freedom. The freedom of democracy is the freedom to make laws and then to have a power behind it to enforce these laws.

Real freedom needs the art of obedience, but to achieve this art we need practice. We can start with our young babies. We play with them the game of stand, of sit. We give the word clearly: Stand! Our gesture shows him what stand means, and as soon as he follows our example we show him our approval. Then we give the order: Sit! Our gesture shows him what sit means. This simple exercise we repeat many times. We also do similar exercises with our older children in school when we practice our verbs—sit, relax, walk, skip, jump, smile, whisper, etc. After these exercises there is a fragrance of happiness, because happiness is the result of achievement, not of having or getting something. Happiness cannot be bought with potato chips or yum yums, even though the skipping, smiling children of the television commercial give us that impression. Happiness is something we have to work for and it is our first task to make the children aware of real happiness.

—MRS. JOHANNES LAVEN

EXPERIENCES AS MONTESSORI TEACHERS IN THE UNITED STATES

Editor's note: In the fall of 1961, Mr. Mario Montessori sent three Dutch Montessori teachers to the Sophia School to add to its staff. Herewith Misses Verschuur, de Munnik, and Biemond give their first impressions of American children.

Our first impression of the American children was that they were not very different from our own European children, but, shortly after starting to work in our own classes, we began to see them from a different perspective.

We were surprised, because they became easily bored and were not very interested in the Montessori materials available in the classroom. Then we discovered the great quantity of toys that American children had in their homes, and we realized why our materials looked very dull and lifeless to them—at first.

However, they gradually found out that there were many secrets hidden in the material; secrets which they could sometimes find out by themselves. After a while they learned that they were not to use any material to which they had not been properly introduced, and this prevented them from misusing it. Because they have learned to use the materials properly, the children now know that they come to school not only to play games, but also—as they so proudly call it themselves—"to work."

EPILOGUE

A REVELATION FOR THE FUTURE

Great movements usually have small beginnings. They come into the world unseen, as a seed, and time is needed for their development. The greater and more original the idea, the longer will be the time necessary for the unfolding of all that lies within it. This is the meaning of Emerson's remark that "an institution is the lengthened shadow of a great man."

Though Montessori is no longer with us, it is quite clear that the development of her work is continuing and taking new forms. It is evident that the original impetus is still very far from being spent, and that her vital principles are still going forth conquering and to conquer. It is equally clear, too, that he would be a rash prophet who would attempt to put a term on their further evolution. Because many of these later developments have taken place in different countries, even in different continents, and among groups of people working in different spheres, it is not easy to get an over-all picture of what has happened, and is still happening, in the Montessori world — still less to judge what is going to happen. That is why diverse ideas are current with regard to the nature and significance of Montessori's work, and of the influence of the movement that goes by her name.

We may divide the various assessments of Montessori's work and its influence into four main groups.

To the general public, the name Montessori suggests little more than a special kind of school for teaching small children — a sort of glorified kindergarten. People have a rather hazy notion that it is a method that has to do with freedom — often, it is thought, with too much freedom, and "letting children do just what they. like."

The average kindergarten teacher has a somewhat better acquaintance with the Montessori method. She has "done" it in her college course, along with other modern methods — Dewey, Froebel, Decroly, the Activity school, etc. She has probably been told that, as a system, it has its good points, but that too much stress is laid upon the Montessori materials — that its principles are too rigid and formal, that Montessori did not believe in fairy tales, and as a consequence her system tends to hinder the free development of the imagination. Further, they may be informed that the method is now outmoded and that what was good in it has already been incorporated in other more up-to-date systems.

Next we come to a third group, better informed and much more penetrating in their evaluation of Montessori's contribution. This includes many psychologists, doctors, biologists and professors of education. These persons realize that Montessori's ideas, taken as a whole, constitute a new and seminal principle in the sphere of education — a sort of leaven which has worked, and still works, far beyond the limits of those schools which call themselves after her name. Typical of this group in England was the late Sir Percy Nunn, former principal of the London Day Training college, who wrote twenty years ago: "It argues no ingratitude to the great name of Froebel and his thousands of devoted followers to connect the new impulse which is everywhere at work in our schools more directly with the doctrine and labors of Maria Montessori than with any other single source."

To this third group also belong many of Dr. Montessori's own followers who have studied her method and now devote their lives to carrying out her principles in Montessori schools in every part of the world. For we must remember that this is an international movement, and centers for the training of Montessori directresses exist in most of the countries of Europe, in places as far away as Delhi and Ceylon, and now in the United States. Before passing on to consider the fourth group, let us note that all those we have mentioned so far have this in common: that they look upon Montessori primarily as someone who has invented a new method of education — the Montessori method.

We now come to the consideration of the fourth group. If we were to ask one of these, "For what achievement will Montessori's name go down in history?", they would answer: "Not because of any revolution in educational method, but because through the work of Montessori there has come into the world *the revelation of the true child, the revelation of hitherto unknown and unsuspected capacities in the soul of the child.*" And with this judgment Montessori would doubtless have agreed. The really significant thing about her work lies in this tremendous fact, demonstrated by herself and her followers again and again in a score of different countries, and beyond all possibility of denial: that, given the right conditions, "children," to use her own words, *"change their character, almost their nature, revealing profound characteristics in their infantile souls which had at first remained unknown. These little children demonstrate to us the interior laws for the formation of men, laws which have given rise to a method of education which has spread throughout the world among every race."*

Unfortunately the stupendous fact of this revelation became confused, and, as it were, overlaid by a disproportionate emphasis on the new method of education which arose out of it. To quote again from Montessori:

"The rational world of adults could not understand the revelations of the children except as a result of a new method of education. And thus, instead of research into the infantile soul, there developed a series of discussions, arid and useless, on the 'New Education.'

"It was not a method which had produced those manifestations so much as the manifestations which had produced the Montessori method — or, better still, had sketched its general outlines. And this first sketch came to be regarded as a talisman. It has, in fact, run the risk of causing this manifestation of new souls to disappear — and to become forgotten under a sea of experiments and errors."

To those then who belong to what we have called above "the fourth group," the Montessori movement stands for something very much wider and deeper than a new method of teaching. For these it represents the beginning of a great new social revolution based on the revelation of the hitherto unknown potentialities of childhood. We are not now thinking of children simply as individuals to be educated, but taken collectively as a creative force to be used for the recreation of civilization — a force which has hitherto never been fully implemented and, when it is, will usher in a new world for a new man.

According to Dr. Montessori, we are living in a critical period in the history of humanity, a period of transition between an epoch which is ending and one which is emerging. Something is wrong with our civilization — a vital factor has been left out. What is it? Montessori's answer is short, clear and definite — the child as a social factor. All the great civilizations of the past, including our own, have been built on an insufficient foundation. The basis on which societies have hitherto been organized has taken into account only the adult values of life. Human civilization will find itself on the right road only when it restores the child to his proper place. Yet "restores" is not really the right word, for up to now there has never been a civilization in which the child has been given his true rights and had the opportunity of exercising due influence in its construction.

Far from being vague or rhetorical, this is a statement as definite as any of Dr. Freud or Einstein. To appreciate what Montessori is getting at, we must learn to look at a familiar thing — childhood — in an unfamiliar way. Let us quote her own words: "The child . . . is a human entity having importance in himself. This is a new and difficult concept and not easy to attain clearly. To do so, in fact, requires an effort of spirit, which must raise us above the plane on which we are accustomed to consider the child, an effort which leads to a more abstract plane on which we are able to find higher values . . .

"The child and the adult are two distinct parts of humanity which must work together and interpenetrate in harmony with reciprocal aid. They are not merely a succession of phases in the individual's life.

"Therefore, it is not only the adult who must aid the child but also the child who must aid the adult. Even more: in the critical moment of history through which we are passing, the assistance of the child has become urgently necessary for all nations.

"Our civilization has been slowly organized from its very origins as if only the adult existed. The evolution of human society has come about solely through the work of the adult. Never that of the child.

"Thus the figure of the child has remained outside our active world, and also outside our mind as we have built up the material form of civilization."

Let us note that an array of new social activities has arisen during the past half century, all of which have the child as their center and inspiration. Nursery schools, infant welfare centers, child guidance clinics, above all UNICEF, witness to this awakened interest in the child. The researches of Freud, Adler, Jung and their followers have emphasized the importance of the early years of childhood, while an increasing number of books have appeared on child psychology.

It would take us far beyond our limits to make even a cursory survey of these movements, but enough has been said to indicate how much justification there is for calling this "the Century of the Child." And this remains true in spite of the fact that, during this same period, civilization has been convulsed by two major world wars.

APPENDIX II

A. BOOKS BY MARIA MONTESSORI

Dr. Montessori's Own Handbook, Introduction by Nancy McCormick Rambusch. Illustrated. Schocken Books, New York, 1965 (cloth and paperbound).

The Montessori Method, Introduction by J. McV. Hunt. Schocken Books, New York, 1964 (cloth and paperbound).

Spontaneous Activity in Education, Introduction by John J. McDermott. Schocken Books, New York, 1965 (cloth and paperbound).

The Montessori Elementary Material. Illustrated. Robert Bentley, Cambridge, Massachusetts, 1964.

The Secret of Childhood. Frederick A. Stokes Company, New York, 1939.

The Absorbent Mind. Illustrated. Theosophical Press, Wheaton, Illinois, 1963.

The Discovery of the Child. Illustrated. Theosophical Press, Wheaton, Illinois, 1962.

Education for a New World. Theosophical Press, Wheaton, Illinois, 1959.

The Formation of Man. Theosophical Press, Wheaton, Illinois, 1962.

To Educate the Human Potential. Theosophical Press, Wheaton, Illinois, 1964.

What You Should Know About Your Child. Theosophical Press, Wheaton, Illinois, 1961.

B. BOOKS ABOUT THE MONTESSORI METHOD

Maria Montessori: Her Life and Work, by E. M. Standing. Academy Guild Press, Fresno, California, 1959.

Montessori for Parents, by Dorothy Canfield Fisher. Illustrated. Robert Bentley, Cambridge, Massachusetts, 1965.

The Montessori Manual for Teachers and Parents, by Dorothy Canfield Fisher. Illustrated. Robert Bentley, Cambridge, Massachusetts, 1965.